John Buyers is a commercial solicitor and partner at Osborne Clarke LLP, an international law firm which specialises in advising high technology or digital business based clients. John manages the UK commercial team and leads Osborne Clarke's international Artificial Intelligence group. He is a frequent commentator on the topic of Artificial Intelligence and the law and speaks regularly both in the UK and internationally on the subject.

John's practice is largely based on transactional IT and outsourcing in the Financial Services sector with a banking and insurance focus. He regularly advises users and suppliers of Artificial Intelligence based systems. John recently concluded a major Asian based financial services outsourcing deal for a global bank which deployed AI technology to verify customer documentation and is currently advising a leading edge provider of an innovative machine learning based insurance risk optimisation tool.

Artificial Intelligence
The Practical Legal Issues

Artificial Intelligence
The Practical Legal Issues

John C. Buyers, LLB Hons, MA
Solicitor England & Wales
and Republic of Ireland
Partner, Head of Commercial,
Osborne Clarke LLP

Law Brief Publishing

Published 2018 by Law Brief Publishing, an imprint of Law Brief Publishing Ltd
30 The Parks
Minehead
Somerset
TA24 8BT

www.lawbriefpublishing.com

Paperback: 978-1-911035-82-4

To Lucy.

ACKNOWLEDGEMENTS

My grateful thanks go to the following people whose helpful thoughts and commentaries proved invaluable in the preparation of this work:

Dr Sanjeev B. Ahuja

Catherine Hammon

PREFACE

The stated law in this book is up to date as at 30th April 2018. Please note that the law relating to artificial intelligence is a new and emerging field. There are a number of ongoing UK and international legislative initiatives which could materially affect the analyses in this book. This work is not intended as a substitute for proper and directed legal advice. In cases of specific query, please consult with your lawyers.

John Buyers
May 2018

CONTENTS

CHAPTER ONE
AN INTRODUCTION TO ARTIFICIALLY INTELLIGENT SYSTEMS

This is a book about technology and artificial intelligence – more specifically one that is designed to assist the non-scientifically minded legal practitioner to understand the implications of this new and exciting technology: to demystify, and hopefully provide clarity around the issues and implications that we as legal practitioners will need to take into account when navigating our disparate legal disciplines. It does not purport to be definitive – the technology is far too new for this and is in a state of constant evolution. What it strives to do is to provide a grounding relative to the current "state of the art" as it applies today, and separate fact from fiction.

We are currently experiencing a golden age or renaissance period for machine learning and wider artificial intelligence based systems. This book is predominantly focussed on the innovations provided by *machine learning* – that is to say technology which, through exponential growth and scale in computing power, has enabled effective use of neural networks to enable machines to adapt and learn *without explicit programming*. It is important however not to ignore associated technologies that complement and enhance machine learning systems, and it is this wider ensemble of techniques (including machine learning itself) which I refer to as *artificial intelligence or AI*.

To the casual observer, it seems that the technology is advancing on a daily or even hourly basis. You can now talk to an Amazon Echo device using the ordinary spoken word (in whatever language is your norm) and through the miracle of natural language processing get a cogent answer, or instruct Google to run context based searches on characteristics gleaned from your photo collection. Facebook will now identify your friends and family for you and Spotify will try to define your musical tastes by selecting music tracks based on your listening history.

We're at the stage now where you can also get into your Tesla vehicle and it will drive you to your destination (albeit with your hands on the wheel). Motoring is an apt analogy, as we accelerate off into a brave new world, cosseted and nannied by ever complex varieties of AI powered gadgets. It's not all about consumer experience though. Financial markets have long been driven by a variety of robo-trading tools and many "state of the art" cyber protection systems use artificial intelligence to protect against an ever-complex world of malware.

What makes these systems different from traditional computer systems and why should we be worried? Sometimes it can be difficult to differentiate fact from fiction – particularly in an environment which is driven by marketing hype and plain old misinformation – especially so given that the idea of the intelligent machine, fuelled by Hollywood, plays heavily on our collective psyche. Is for example artificial intelligence the end of the world as we know it and are we about to be suborned to a new species of supercomputer, or is it the key to a prosperous new future and a golden age of human endeavour ? This book will at least give you an oversight of the issues involved from a legal perspective, and I suspect an appreciation that the reality is somewhat more prosaic than either the pessimists or optimists would have us believe.

In order to understand the practical implications of the technology, it is worth understanding how traditional computer systems work, and analogise this against how neuroscience currently thinks that neurons in the human brain function.

Computers in the traditional sense need prescriptive and directive sets of instructions to execute complex tasks – in essence, their programming. A traditional computer is unable to handle complex tasks effectively unless every eventuality is programmed into its code. As we all know, this makes these machines highly effective at larger repetitive or data intensive tasks, with a defined set of pre-programmed variables. What such machines cannot do well is adapt, learn, evolve or extrapolate their decisions to new and unforeseen situations. In contrast, the human brain although rather less good at repetitive tasks, is a marvel of flexibility and of navigating through a chaotic world. It does this through a process of *conceptualisation*.

The simple act of recognising a human face (or indeed any image) provides a real-life example. You learn from an early age as a human being to recognise a face from any angle or orientation, full on or profile. You can identify someone in low light conditions and you don't need an image of a face to be in colour or even in three dimensions for you to recognise it. Your brain can extrapolate a face from incomplete or partial data – indeed it is unbelievably good at "joining the dots" (so much so that we are often caught out by recognising anthropomorphic features in inanimate objects). A traditionally programmed computer finds this task almost insurmountably complex and difficult to achieve. You need to ensure that the face you want the machine to recognise is oriented in precisely the right way and under precisely the right lighting conditions – as otherwise it may not even identify it as a face. In this context, what the human neo-cortex achieves (and what current AI technologists are trying to replicate) is the holy grail of the "*invariant representation*". This is the ability to learn what a "face" is as a *concept* (or indeed a cube, car, tree or any other animate or inanimate thing) and apply this to real world data. The notion of a concept introduces an entirely new dimension – a level of data abstraction, classification, recognition and labelling which enables semantic representation in areas such as pattern recognition and linguistics, in short, bringing order from chaos.

Put grandly, artificially intelligent systems aspire through their struc- tures (to a greater or lesser degree) to have the ability to process unstructured data, to extrapolate it, and to adapt and evolve in ways which are comparable to human beings.

Robotics, perception and Artificial Intelligence

So what makes robots different from machine learning systems? It is worth briefly covering the difference as to the uninitiated, this can be a somewhat confusing question – particularly when the terms are used fast, loose and interchangeably in most commercial, non-technical literature.

Obviously, at its most simplistic level, a robot is a mechanism that is designed to replicate the actions and behaviours of living creatures. It is a manufactured autonomous agent in the real world which is capable of autonomous action to a defined degree. Robots in some form or another have been in existence for over 200 years.

As AI systems have become more sophisticated and able, robotic research has likewise developed more capable robotic machines and scientists in the field of robotics have become more pre-occupied with replicating animal characteristics of proprioception –the unconscious ability in living creatures of knowing at all times the boundaries and extent of their physical body and that when a limb is extended in front of it, it is part of its own body and has a sense of movement. Knowing also that the limb is sensing hot or cold or touching another object, and whether it is constrained or injured are an integral part of this ability in living creatures. It is this need to physically interact with the real world on an effective basis which has been described by some commentators as one of the primary catalysts of animal and human intelligence and which is the driving emphasis for AI research in the field of robotics.

A brief history of AI

Before we get into how current "state of the art" artificially intelligent systems are structured, it is worth (briefly) looking at the historical evolution of machine learning. It was Alan Turing who first coined the term "artificial intelligence", and who through his brilliant efforts in the second world war, managed to decode Nazi Germany ciphers produced on the Enigma machine. Alan Turing wrote on the concept of machine intelligence in a seminal 1950 paper[1]. His analysis centred on human intelligence as a benchmark for artificial intelligence (more on this

---

1 Computing Machinery and Intelligence (1950) by A.M. Turing

later). He postulated that if you could hold a test where a human conversed with a computer and that human could be fooled by a clever computer program into thinking that the machine they were talking to was in fact human, then the machine would have passed a benchmark for intelligence. This of course evolved into the famous "*Turing test*".

The Turing test led to a surge in the mid 20th century in traditional programming techniques being used to emulate intelligence – however developers very soon realised the limitations of this approach. Programs such as Eliza, one of the very first early winners of a Turing test, fooled reviewers by adopting clever, but simple linguistic tricks (e.g. through the repetition of questions) which gave a superficial semblance of self-awareness and interaction through mimicry but did not create anything approaching human equivalent intelligence. Unsurprisingly AI development stagnated after these initial attempts.

The father of AI is rightly credited to be Marvin Minsky, an American cognitive research scientist who developed the first randomly wired neural network learning machine, SNARC[2] in January 1952. Minsky was also author of the book *Perceptrons* (with Seymour Papert) in 1969 that became a seminal work in the field of artificial neural networks.

For the purposes of this book I am of course paraphrasing a long and complex developmental history – there are many works which espouse the historical evolution of artificial intelligence in a much greater depth but it was subsequent to the development of the Turing test that AI research bifurcated into two distinct directions. One of which centred on the earlier approach of "emulation" – namely focussing on mimicking outwardly observable intelligent behaviours; and a new approach of "simulation" – one which was based on the view that in order to achieve machine intelligence the fundamental structure and processes of neurons firing in the human nervous system had to be simulated.

As we shall see later on, both branches of research are propelling AI development through its current renaissance. There are however still

---

2 Stochastic neural analog reinforcement calculator

limitations. Not least due to the fact that despite much scientific endeavour, we are still a very long way off from understanding precisely how the human brain functions, and for this reason, probably a long way off from developing a machine with human equivalent (or greater) levels of sentience (or feeling, perception and subjective experience), combined with objective reasoning and logic – the holy grail of *Artificial General Intelligence (AGI)* or "*Strong AI*".

Inevitably, AI research and development initiatives have themselves evolved and differentiated themselves by trial and error – as some structures have shown promise, those have been refined, so now we have lines of machine learning research and applications which may in fact have very little relationship to how neuroscience currently understands the organisation and structure of the human brain (in addition of course to those that still strive to closely model real organic brain function in so far as it is understood).

Current developments

So let's now take a slightly more detailed look at what is actually happening in the field of artificial intelligence at the moment – both from the perspectives of the technology itself and also the wider political and industry context which is providing an ethical and regulatory response to these developments.

As I mentioned at the beginning of this chapter, we have seen a dramatic rise in the effectiveness and use of solutions based on "*Weak AI*" or "*Narrow AI*" or *Artificial Specific Intelligence (ASI)* – AI solutions that are based around a specific, narrowly defined task or application, collectively (and somewhat confusingly) falling under the umbrella term of *IA* or *Intelligent Automation*.

There are several real-world artificial intelligence applications which are driving developments in the technology:

Image processing and tagging

Image processing as it suggests requires algorithms to analyse images to get data or to perform transformations. Examples of this include identification/image tagging – as used in applications such as Facebook to provide facial recognition or to ascertain other data from a visual scan, such as health of an individual or location recognition for geodata; Optical Character Recognition – where algorithms learn to read handwritten text and convert documents into digital versions.

3D Environment processing

3D environment processing is an extension of the image processing and tagging skill – most obviously translated into the skills required by an algorithm in a robot or a "CAV" (connected and autonomous vehicle) to spatially understand its location and environment. This uses image data but also potentially radar and lidar sourced spatial scanning data to process 3D geometries. Typically this technology could also be used in free roaming robot devices including pilotless drones.

Textual Analysis

These are techniques and algorithms which extract information from or classify textual data. Textual analysis uses two distinct approaches – one based purely on pattern recognition of words and their meanings and concatenated sequences of the same, the other on grammar driven natural language processing. In terms of practical usage, these could include social media postings, tweets or emails. The technology may then be used to provide filtering (for SPAM); information extraction – for example to pull out particular pieces of data such as names and addresses or more complex "sense based" sentiment analysis – to identify the mood of the person writing (as Facebook has recently implemented in relation to postings by members who may be potentially suicidal[3]). Text analysis is also at the heart of Chatbot technology – allowing for interaction on social media, or providing for automated first line technical support.

Speech Analysis

Speech processing takes equivalent skills to those used for textual documents and applies them to the spoken word. It is this area which is seeing an incredible level of investment in the creation of personal digital home assistants from the likes of Amazon (with its Echo device), Microsoft with Cortana, Google's Home device and Apple with Siri (and now the recently launched "Homepod" speaker).

Data Mining

This is the process of discovering patterns or extrapolating trends from data. Data mining algorithms are used for such things as Anomaly detection – identifying for example fraudulent entries or transactions as outliers or classifying them as known types of fraud; Association rules – detecting supermarket purchasing habits by looking at a shopper's typical shopping basket; and Predictions – predicting a variable from a set of others to extrapolate for example a credit score.

Video game virtual environment processing

Video games are a multi-billion dollar entertainment industry but they are also key sandboxes for machines to interact with and learn behaviours in relation to other elements in a virtual environment, including interacting with the players themselves[4].

3　See for example http://www.bbc.co.uk/news/technology-39126027 "Facebook artificial intelligence spots suicidal users", 1st March 2017

4　See for example the July edition (E308) knowledge feature of Edge Magazine – "Machine Language" which discusses new startup SpiritAI – a business that has

Machine Learning – the basic elements

At the most simplistic level, machine learning systems are no different from conventional computer systems in that both rely on the elements of computational hardware and software to function effectively.

Whilst many modern machine learning systems exploit huge advances in computing scale and power and make use of the vast amounts of data that are available in our "big data" society, they still need what would be recognisable as a computing platform. It is the logic or software that such systems use which differs markedly from traditional computer programs directly created by human programmers which require sequential, explicit and largely linear instructions that are followed to the letter by the machine.

I have already explained that technologists developing machine learning systems have developed a variety of solutions, methodologies, models and structures to get machines to "*think*" in a narrow AI sense. In fact so many approaches have been developed, it can be difficult for the non-computer scientist to effectively decode them. To further complicate this issue, many proprietary machine learning systems employ a "mix" of adaptive learning solutions which are optimised for the particular applications at hand. We'll step through some of these models in a moment, but for the moment, and in order to provide a consistent framework for you, the reader, it is worth setting out the very basic absolutes of machine learning systems – in other words, those conceptual elements that *all* current machine learning systems use. It is important to stress that this framework applies to that subset of AI which is *machine learning* as defined at the beginning of this chapter – the terms may not be relevant to other wider or peripheral AI technologies which are generally out of scope for the purposes of this book.

---

developed an intelligent character engine for NPCs (non-player characters) in video games, thus obviating the need for thousands of pages of pre-scripted dialogue.

At the most simplistic level It is generally established that machine learning systems are comprised of three parts: the *Model* – that is to say the way in which the system is structured and organised – in short its architecture, including the nodes, links and weights which will be applied to the data to be processed. Then there are the *Parameters* – these are the properties of the training data that are to be learned during training and finally the *Learner* –generally comprised of a *learning algorithm* that part of the system that adjusts the model for how it processes the parameters on a *supervised, unsupervised* or *reinforcement* basis (see below under "*Training*") and an *activation or transfer algorithm* which defines the way in which data are to be transferred between nodes within the network by forwards and or backwards propagation (see further below under "*Backpropagation*").

Algorithms

The word "*algorithm*" is often used to generalise the entire process I have described above. In many texts you might as well substitute the words for "*magic spell*". In fact, as we have seen above, an algorithm is merely a set of complex mathematical actions expressed as a formula. Clearly machine learning algorithms are not magic spells. More prosaically, learning algorithms selectively adapt and change the model and parameters based on the data that is introduced into the machine learning system. Rather confusingly as well, it is important to note (and often misunderstood), that simply referring to a solution that is "*algorithmic*" does not necessarily imply that that solution has any degree of artificial intelligence or machine learning.

Training

All machine learning systems need to be "*trained*" (or train themselves) with a data set – a set of data points which are intended to assist the system to "understand" the relevant narrow AI task at hand and which contain the parameters I have described above. Training data sets are, as we shall see later on in this book, an incredibly significant and important feature of these systems. The nature of the training data set provided however is very different depending upon whether the system is designed to learn on a *"supervised"*, *"unsupervised"* or *"reinforcement"* basis.

Supervised Learning

Supervised learning systems are provided with guiding or labelled training data sets that contain a mass of examples of the desired answers and outputs. In such cases, the training data are subsets of data that are well known in terms of all of their features, content, correlations and so forth and thus can provide a good representative example to benchmark the outputs of the system. Typically these data sets will be past, real life examples of the problem the system has been configured to resolve. Typically, this type of machine learning supports evaluation, classification or prediction outcomes.

Unsupervised Learning

Systems that are designed to learn on an unsupervised basis in contrast are provided with unlabelled data that may or may not contain the desired answer or output. In these cases, the systems attempt to find either outliers or correlations or patterns in the data without any form of guidance. Provided data sets may be clustered into different classes that share some common characteristics – unsurprisingly, this is often referred to as "clustering" by the industry. Typically, this type of machine learning is found in forensic tools.

Reinforcement Learning

Reinforcement learning is a similar process to unsupervised learning – however machine learning systems here are typically exposed to a competitive environment where they train themselves continuously using trial and error to try to find the best reward – which might be winning a game or earning more money. This type of AI system attempts to learn from past experience in order to refine and improve decision outcomes, and is particularly well suited to closed environments with static rules

Whether the system is designed to work on a supervised or unsupervised basis it is clearly vitally important that the data sets provided to train the system need to be representative of the underlying problem the system is being designed to resolve and should not be unbalanced or skewed in any particular direction. As we'll see later on in this book, there are particular issues with this which could trap the unwary. Proactively editing out bias too far in a data set may well have the opposite and undesired effect of making that data set too specific (so called "*overfitting*") and less representative of the data class, in turn leading to the corresponding outputs of the system being prejudiced in favour of or against particular outcomes.

Backpropagation

Backpropagation is the process which allows a machine learning system to adjust and change by reference to previous outcomes. In technical terms it is the means by which the machine learning system (via the *activation algorithm*, see above) computes and optimises the gradient descent required in the calculation of weights used in the network by distributing *back* through network nodes.

So these are the basic features of AI or machine learning systems. As I mentioned above, there are a variety of different AI *Models* which are being deployed, and it is worth spending a little time on the most significant of these.

Artificial Neural Networks

Artificial neural networks aim to most closely model the functioning of the human brain through the simulation approach and contain all of the basic machine learning elements described above.

Neuroscience has established that the human neo-cortex, which is where most of our higher brain function resides, consists of a very dense population of interconnected neurons or brain cells. Neurons consist of the soma (the cell body) and axons and dendrites (the filaments that extend from the cell itself). Observed higher human brain functions require groups or networks of neurons to fire together in electro chemical activity. Even though the base physical structure of the cortex is the same, it is settled science that there are cortical regions that specialise in particular skills, such as language, motor movement, sight and hearing. More recently, it has been established that there are progressively "higher" levels of brain processing driven by layers of neurons. You might for example have a collection of neurons at a low level that are specialised in the visual detection of "edges". Data from these lower functions is passed up the tree (or network) to higher functions so that collectively, you are able to perceive a face.

In the world of artificial intelligence, scientists have attempted to replicate or model these structures and their functionality by use of neural networks. In simplistic terms, neural networks can be organised as "shallow" – 1-3 layers or "deep" – over 7 layers (as is generally the case in the human neo-cortex).

Artificial neural networks are composed of artificial input "neurons" – virtual computing "cells" that *activate*, that is to say, assume a numeric value (by reference to a chosen algorithm which applies weights and biases to that numeric value – in effect influencing it) and then hand it off to another layer of the network, which also applies an algorithmic treatment to it, and so on and so forth until the data has passed through the entire network and is outputted.

The process is heavily mathematical. Most neural networks apply something called a *cost function*, which is an additional mathematical process that determines how to adjust the network's weights and biases in order to make it more accurate. Typically this is achieved by something called *gradient descent* – a calculus derived mathematical function which is designed to reach the *minima* (the lowest possible, and hence the most accurate value, of the *cost function* described above).

Stepping away from the maths for a moment, it is worth making the point that Artificial Neural Networks process data in a non-linear manner – as we saw from the basic elements section above, data may *backpropagate* as well as move forwards through the network (a further mathematically driven process of output refinement and tuning). They are often therefore referred to as "*black boxes*". This can make it very difficult to understand and equally difficult to explain how or why the system has reached a particular outcome in a particular instance.

It is also important to note that neural networks come in a variety of flavours, so for example **Regression Neural Networks** are neural networks that are trained to analyse data on either a linear or non-linear regression basis (a simple example of regression analysis might be extrapolating growth rates from height measurements taken from a child).

Convolutional Neural Networks or ("**CNNs**") have a structure which is specifically optimised for image recognition (such networks assume that all inputs are image related). **Generative Adversarial Networks** take this one step further and improve applications such as image recognition and optimisation by pitting one CNN against another. One network acts as image generator, the other acts as image discriminator, challenging the generating network to improve. Use of this technique has proved very valuable in picture enhancement – such as for example improving the resolution of fuzzy images or removing artefacts.

GANs are also particularly effective where no correlated data exists to underpin decisions relating to a processing application – in other words, it can be used to synthesise data where none actually exist. One particular company for example uses such an approach to synthesise claims data for insurers to enable them to more accurately model and price risk for the underwriting process.

Deep Learning Networks

Deep learning models are simply varieties of artificial neural networks that employ vastly greater computing power, more recent algorithmic innovations and much bigger data sets – in short, they take advantage of the much greater computing power available to us, but operate in much the same manner as I have described above. Of course, the challenges of explainability and transparency are also correspondingly amplified when such networks are used.

On a wider basis, it is probably worth providing a brief introduction to some other non-machine learning AI technologies, although I do not propose to delve into these in any great detail.

Decision Trees

In contrast to machine learning, decision trees are a "*white box*" artificial intelligence model – typically their decisions are more easily explicable and they are principally used for classification style problems. In simple terms a decision tree works by processing data through a series of question "nodes" (similar to a flow diagram type structure). Each node hands off data to corresponding next layer once a question has been answered. Decision trees usually work on a Boolean basis (ie *yes* or *no*). Decision trees depend upon being able to classify data sets in an expected manner and are not suitable for applications that are based on unsupervised pattern correlation or recognition. This means that they are in turn susceptible to in-built bias if the overall problem they are designed to resolve has been incorrectly modelled.

Random Forests

Random Forests and Deep Forests are very large ensembles of Decision Trees. In simple terms, Random Forests take random subsets of data to be analysed and assign these to individual trees. The collective output of the trees provides a range of responses which can be correlated on a statistical basis to provide a stronger prediction than a single decision tree alone. I do not propose to explain the intricacies of these structures further in this book, however the reader should note that by aggregating decision trees together in a very large hierarchy, such structures may become inherently less explicable in terms of their decision making.

Probabilistic artificial intelligence

Probabilistic or Bayesian artificial intelligence techniques are some of the hardest to conceptualise and understand. They may or may not incorporate machine learning technology. Systems that work on this basis are attempting, by application of mathematical probability theory, to express all forms of uncertainty associated with the problem the model is trying to resolve. They then apply inverse probability (*Bayes' Rule*) to infer unknown characteristics of the problem to make predictions about, and learn from observed data (so called "*inference algorithms*").

The greatest strength of Probabilistic models is that they *know what they do not know* or in effect have an internal representation of past outcomes that are learned, on the basis of which they can guess a probable outcome. We live and work in a very messy world – and many decisions we take are inferred from observable data sets that are incomplete. Such systems are therefore incredibly powerful but do depend on a very careful probabilistic representation of uncertainty.

So that was an introduction to the key elements of the technology. In so far as political, regulatory and industry responses are concerned, there are a number that are worth mentioning, as they reflect well some of the issues and concerns raised in this book.

The Partnership on AI

The first, and possibly the most significant is the Partnership on AI or "PAI"[5] which has been established between Google, Microsoft, Apple, Amazon, IBM and Facebook (together with a number of other leading industry participants). The PAI attempts broadly to ensure that industry leaders in the development of AI do so on an ethical basis, taking into account a number of thematic "pillars" or priorities. These pillars include establishing conventions for safety in the use of AI and robotic systems (a key element of which is ensuring that AI systems cede gracefully when they fail rather than putting the user in a catastrophic position); making AI fair, transparent and accountable (in order to increase the auditability of decisions taken by AI systems); promoting co-operative AI systems; and variously considering the extent to which AI will influence society to ensure that it is for the greater good. Obviously it remains to be seen how influential this partnership will be in practice.

OpenAI

OpenAI[6] is a non-profit AI research company which is focussed on developing AGI or artificial general intelligence. OpenAI, which was founded in 2015 jointly by entrepreneurs Sam Altman and Elon Musk, has been set up to counteract the concentrative effect of big corporation research into AI technologies and to ensure that AGI will ultimately benefit all of humanity. As at the date of writing of this book, OpenAI is intending to release a charter of principles in relation to the development of AGI.

---

5 See www.partnershiponai.org

6 https://openai.com

The EU

The EU is currently undertaking a complex review of the impact of artificial intelligence on European Society, which includes a number of strategic initiatives. At this stage, the most that can be done is to indicate direction of travel – but one thing is for certain – this is a fast-moving area and it is very likely that by the time this work is published, much of the information listed will be out of date. The significance of the technology to the EU is clear – it has been awarded its own Unit within the Directorate General for Communication Networks, Content and Technology of the EU Commission. There are a number of research initiatives, the most significant of which are SPARC[7] – a €2.2bn public-private partnership on Robotics in the EU (partially funded by the EU as part of its Horizon 2020 funding programme which covers expenditure between 2014-2020), and a €20m "AI On Demand" Platform initiative on standardisation – the stated and rather ambitious aims for which are to *"mobilise the AI community across Europe in order to combine efforts and to optimise Europe's potential."* Further details from this programme are expected in April 2018 from the Commission.

In March 2018, the European Group on Ethics in Science and New Technologies, part of the European Commission's Directorate General for Research and Innovation, published its *"Statement on Artificial Intelligence, Robotics and 'Autonomous' Systems"*[8] which advocates the creation of an ethical and legal framework for the design, production, use and governance of artificial intelligence, robotics and autonomous systems, as well as proposing a set of fundamental ethical principles for the development of AI which are consistent with the EU's charter of fundamental rights.

---

7 https://eu-robotics.net/sparc/

8 9th March 2018, ISBN 978-92-7980328-4

The UK

The UK has been keen to remain at the forefront of Artificial Intelligence development and research. In October 2017 an independent review commissioned by the UK government was published by Dame Wendy Hall and Jerome Presenti *"Growing the Artificial Intelligence Industry in the UK"*[9]. The review made a number of recommendations about how the UK could best exploit new technologies created by Artificial Intelligence (principally in the areas of skills, driving uptake, data security and research) and is currently being considered as part of the UK government's Industrial Strategy programme. This was followed in April 2018 by a wide ranging report by the House of Lords Select Committee on Artificial Intelligence entitled *"AI in the UK; ready, willing and able?"*[10], two of the main recommendations of which were to suggest that the AI industry set up a voluntary mechanism to inform consumers when AI is being used to make significant and sensitive decisions about individual consumers, and to ask the Law Commission to provide clarity in areas of the law where there is uncertainty around the consequences of artificial intelligence systems malfunctioning, underperforming or making decisions which cause harm.

---

9 Available online at the Department for Digital, Culture, Media and Sport website

10 HL Paper 100, 16th April 2018

CHAPTER TWO
CAUSATION AND ARTIFICIAL INTELLIGENCE

AI Liability: A Sliding Scale

Liability is essentially a scalable concept which is based factually on the degree of legal responsibility society places on a *person*. As we will see later on, historically responsibility and hence liability levels are not static – the able-minded, children and mentally incapable adults all have different levels of liability – the latter having little or no responsibility for their actions and therefore a commensurately lower level of account-ability and liability.

The degree to which an artificially intelligent system could in theory assume responsibility for its actions thus depends, from a philosophical perspective (and taking aside any need to amend the law to account for such liability), on the extent to which it is aware of those actions. In the previous chapter, we saw that the current state of the art is providing us with some very clever discrete (or narrow) solutions to particular problems. This does not yet equate however to human levels of sen-tience or even self-awareness.

Until relatively recently, the question of whether or not a machine should be accountable and hence liable for its actions was a relatively trite one – a machine was merely a tool of the person using or operating it. There was absolutely no question of machines assuming a level of personal accountability or even "*personhood*" as they were incapable of autonomous or semi-autonomous action. This is essentially the way in which the law has evolved to deal with machine generated con-sequences.

We are now however poised to deal with how to creatively twist our liability frameworks so as to account for the consequences created by autonomous machine action. Before we get into a discussion of existing liability frameworks, it is worth exploring this sliding scale theme. With this in mind, future liability frameworks are going to need to differen-tiate between traditional "dumb" machines at the one end, and super-intelligent semi or fully sentient machines at the other end.

A "*HAL 9000*" sentient supercomputer will have a greater degree of autonomy, independent thought and hence greater consequences coming from its action, and when it is created is very likely to be imbued with some form of personhood. In a sense, the two ends of the spectrum are easy to rationalise – the real conundrum is dealing with the liability consequences of a machine sandwiched between the HAL 9000 and the toaster: one which has properties of independent and autonomous action but not the clear attributes of a person as we under-stand it.

Complexity – A causative blocker

Taking aside the degree to which an AI system can assume awareness for its actions, there is a rather more immediate problem in the usage of current AI systems which is driven by the legal concept of *causation*. We will look at existing liability frameworks shortly, but put simply, in order to establish liability you need to demonstrate that the person or thing *caused* the relevant loss or damage.

Existing causative liability models work well when machine functions (and hence responses) can by and large be traced back to human design, programming and knowledge.

In machine learning systems this is usually very difficult to achieve espe-cially in artificial neural networks or probabilistic Bayesian networks where computer scientists are often unable to determine how or why (on a human explicable basis) a machine learning system has made a particular decision.

The current "*state of the art*" does not provide for systems to self-report their decisions, but there is a widely held view in the relevant scientific community that regulators will force developers to interject "explanation systems" into their AI solutions where they are deployed in envir-onments where their outputs (or decisions) are likely to have a significant regulatory or human impact such as healthcare or financial services.

There are technical concerns however that these explanation systems may impair or limit the operation of the core machine learning system (by constraining them to a narrower spectrum of decisions that are human explicable) and may be of limited use where the rationale or decision adopted by the ML system is not capable of human explan-ation. As noted earlier, probabilistic Bayesian networks and artificial neural networks are particularly difficult to decipher owing to their structures – decision trees may be slightly easier (decision tree networks that are organised into Random Forests may however regain "*black box*" characteristics).

Interestingly, there is a current theoretical view that distributive, decentralised blockchain technology may provide the ideal character-istics for an auditable framework for such explanation systems by underpinning and logging in an immutable way each step of the arti-ficial reasoning process – however we are some distance from any such auditing technology being introduced in practical terms.

Aside from the question of whether a decision is traceable from a caus-ative viewpoint, it may also be incorrect to classify an undesired decision or "learned behaviour" adopted by a machine learning system as subjectively wrong – just because a system produces an undesirable result does not mean it is defective. AI systems are renowned for what are known as their "*edge case*" decisions – those decisions which are at the margins of the probability curve for their operating parameters. Much scientific effort is devoted to tuning out these edge cases, but they still occur (indeed in some cases these outcomes may be positively encouraged).

Existing liability frameworks

So, with this in mind, let's review the existing liability frameworks which could conceivably apply to what are termed "*machine generated consequences*". Current liability frameworks are focussed on product liability generally – broken down into three distinct categories: Contract law, Negligence (tort) and, so far as the UK (and EU) is concerned, strict liability under consumer protection legislation (in the UK the Consumer Protection Act 1987).

We'll review the scope of each briefly in a moment and then consider potential issues in relation to their application to AI systems. In this context, the most conventional analysis we can apply to intelligent or semi-intelligent machines is as complex products.

Using the driverless car as an example, what we can see is that in fact it is an assemblage of many and varied integrated systems that are produced by multiple manufacturers. For a driverless car to work effectively, it needs sensors to navigate road obstructions, such as radar and lidar detection. It must have a computer to direct its actions and that computer needs to have a logic framework within which to operate – internally by use of its own operating software and also externally by reference to map data. All of these systems need to work together effectively, and this is without consideration of all the usual mechanical components which form a standard car, which must also be present and functioning.

Taking aside the organisational complexity of the AI system itself which we have already discussed, this mechanical complexity alone gives rise to a potential plethora of liability targets, ranging from the vehicle manufacturer itself, all the way down to the designer of an individual component, depending upon where the actual defect, fault or breach occurs.

Contract

Contract clearly has a role to play in determining product-based liability. Contracts ensure that manufacturers and retailers sell products that meet agreed pre-determined standards. Such liability is obviously aimed at the recovery of financial (or pure economic) loss as a result of breach of these contractual standards, however obviously, as we are all aware, contract liability can in some circumstances lead to the recovery of damages for consequential loss.

Contract terms and hence liability may be either express – as to defects and warranties or implied. In the UK there are implied terms as to quality, fitness for purpose, title and description in the Consumer Rights Act 2015 so far as B2C contracts are concerned and the Sale of Goods Act 1979 for B2B contracts. Although there is not a focus on "*defects*" per se under the Sale of Goods legislation, there is clearly an emphasis on conformity with description. Arguably that could amount to nearly the same thing: a failure to conform to a description or specification is very close to a "*defect*" in practical terms.

We'll take a look at the relevant strengths and weaknesses of contract liability in this context in a moment, but it is worth remembering that contract is a *causative* based liability framework. In order to found liability, the Claimant must prove that there was a breach of either an express or an implied term and that that breach caused the loss. Contract causation is often overlooked as the poor cousin of tort causation but ever since the time of *Hadley v. Baxendale[1]*, it is still a relevant factor in determining liability. This is an important factor – and again one we'll return to later.

Finally, it is worth remembering that the primary remedy for breach of contract is damages (as assessed to put the innocent party in the position they would have been had the contract been correctly performed). The primary advantage of contract liability is of course that it is open to the contract counterparties to determine the scope of the contract

---

1 [1854] EWHC J70

responsibilities and obligations as between them and hence the liability if things do go wrong. This means that it is quite open to tailor the agreement to the functions and performance of the AI system involved.

So far as the implied terms are concerned, Section 9 of the Consumer Rights Act provides that where goods are sold "in the course of a business" there is an implied term that the goods are of *satisfactory quality*[2] and *fit for a purpose*[3] that the buyer has made known to the seller. Products are therefore of satisfactory quality if they meet the standard that a reasonable person would regard as satisfactory, taking into account their description, price and all other relevant circumstances. In other words it could be argued that contract implied terms create a consumer expectation test.

The major disadvantage of contract liability of course is that it is not a liability that applies generally to the "whole world" but rather is one which is constrained by *contract privity* (albeit with limited exceptions in some jurisdictions – such as the Contract (Rights of Third Parties) Act 1999 in the UK).

This means that obligations can only be enforced by contract counterparties. Of course – in some situations it is possible to conceive of a contract relationship subsisting in your use of an intelligent systems – but equally speaking in many others, there will not be. Aside from this, there is a lack of consistency in contractual standards in relation to contracts for the sale of goods which make the application of the framework complex. So, for example, for public policy reasons there are higher standards which apply to contracts made with consumers – the Consumer Rights Act requires that in assessing whether products are of satisfactory quality that account is taken of any "*public statements on the specific characteristics of the goods made about them by the Seller or the producer, particularly in advertising*"[4].

---

2 s9

3 s10

4 s9(5)

Tort

Product liability in tort refers to a breach of a duty of care in negligence. Since the seminal case of ***Donoghue v. Stevenson***[5], tortious duties can run concurrently with contractual liabilities. The essence of the case was that if a consumer purchases products in a form intended to reach him or her without the possibility of reasonable intermediate examination and with the knowledge on the part of the producer that the absence of reasonable care in the preparation of the product will result in personal injury or property damage, which is reasonably foreseeable, then that producer owes a duty to take reasonable care in their production. ***Donoghue v. Stevenson*** concerned decomposed snails in ginger beer bottles but it does not take much to extrapolate that analysis to a driverless car or a surgical robot.

Again, it is worth pointing out the causative nature of tort as a liability framework – it is essentially fault based. The claimant must prove that the defendant owed him or her a duty of care, they failed in that standard and damage was caused as a result.

In contrast to contractual damages, tort-based damages are awarded on the basis of putting the injured party in the position they would have been had the tort not occurred. The scope of potential liability in tort is wide. It could equally apply to manufacturers, producers and anyone directly involved in the manufacture and distribution of a product with a defect. You do however need to establish that a duty of care subsists and was breached – and irrespective of this that the relevant chain of causation is not broken by the damage being too remote.

There are a number of disadvantages with this liability framework – and it is worth pointing them out briefly. There are very real difficulties in claiming damages for pure economic loss in tort – certainly so far as the UK is concerned, and since the high watermark of ***Junior Books v.***

---

5 [1932] AC 562

Veitchi[6], there are only a limited number of circumstances where this is possible, including for example, negligent advice from surveyors.

Contributory negligence can also act as a defence to liability, if it is shown that the claimant should have known of the defect but negligently failed to recognise it or negligently used the product or failed to take account of its operating instructions. In such cases damages are reduced to a degree which is commensurate with the claimant's negligence.

Volenti non fit injuria – or voluntary assumption of risk is less common in product liability cases – on the basis that if a claimant knows of the defect they are less likely to use it and if they do, that usually breaks the causative chain between defect and damage.

As we have seen, as intelligent machines and AI systems "learn" for themselves, their behaviours are increasingly less and less directly attributable to human programming. These machines are not acting on a prescriptive instruction set, but a system of rules that may not have anticipated the precise circumstances under which the machine should act. To take our prior example of the autonomous vehicle, what if our car has been programmed to look after and preserve the safety of its occupants and also to avoid pedestrians at all costs and is placed in an unavoidable situation where it has to make a decision as to whether to avoid a pedestrian crossing into its path (and thereby run into a brick wall, injuring or even killing its occupants) or running over the pedestrian (and thereby saving its occupants). Can any outcome of that decision be said to be a failure or a defect – even if people are injured or possibly killed as a result?

In tort, the doctrine of *res ipsa loquitur* – or the thing speaks for itself assists in providing a partial solution to the problem. The doctrine is equally applicable in the US and the UK.

---

6 [1983] 1 AC 520

Res ipsa loquitur is useful in dealing with cases where there are multiple successive inexplicable failures which cannot in themselves be readily explained. A classic example of the application of this was in the US case of ***Toyota Motor Corporation***[7], where Toyota found that for no particular reason, many of its high-end Lexus model cars simply accelerated – despite the intervention of their drivers. After extensive investigation, the cause of these failures could not be pinpointed by the manufacturer. Toyota took the step of settling 400 pending case against it after an Oklahoma jury applied the doctrine *of res ipsa loquitur* and awarded the plaintiffs in that case $3m in damages.

In the UK the principles are enshrined in the leading case of ***Scott and Bennett v Chemical Construction (GB) Ltd***[8]. This provides for a three-step test for the principle to be applied: (i) the event or accident would not ordinarily have occurred in the absence of negligence (ii) the thing causing the damage must be under the control of the defendant and (iii) there is no evidence as to the cause of the event or accident. Clearly such a test will need to be considered in the context of artificially intelligent machines and the extent to which such a device can be considered to be "under the control" of its user when it is making decisions on its own behalf will be debateable to a greater or lesser degree. What this doctrine also does not provide a solution to of course is the inexplicable *isolated* incident.

Finally, it should be emphasised that on a factual basis, proving liability in tort can be very difficult – especially in product liability cases, as very often the details that are required to show liability are held by the defendant. Obviously there are mechanisms in litigation to get hold of that information – but typically a defendant will not go out of the way to disclose it and might use any number of established disclosure tricks to bury the key facts or at least make them very difficult to ascertain.

---

7 (2013) WL 5763178 (Texas)

8 [1971] 3 All ER 822

Strict Liability: Consumer Protection

The Consumer Protection Act 1987 ("CPA") implements the EU directive on Liability for Defective Products[9]. This Act introduces a strict liability regime which does not affect the general availability of Contract and Tort based remedies. What the Act provides is that a person who is injured or whose personal property is damaged by a product will be able to claim against a manufacturer or supplier of that product (and certain other third parties) if it can be shown that the product was defective.

There is no requirement to prove fault on the part of the manufacturer but obviously there is a requirement on the claimant to show that the defect existed on the preponderance of the evidence. The Act introduces a consumer expectations test in that a defect exists where *"the safety of the product is not such as persons generally are entitled to expect"*[10]. Consumer expectations themselves are subject to a reasonableness test.

In terms of the advantages of the CPA regime – as previously discussed – there is no requirement to show fault; neither is there a privity requirement – the regime itself allows for a wide variety of potential liability targets, including suppliers and manufacturers.

There are still some problems with consumer protection product liability however – obviously causation still exists – although it is limited to the finding of defects and moderated by a consumer expectation test. Furthermore, the Act is designed to cover claims for real damage, so does not encompass claims for pure economic loss.

In the context of artificial intelligence, there are also problems with the definition of *"Product"* under the Act. Product is defined as *"any goods or electricity and includes products aggregated into other products, whether as component parts, raw materials or otherwise"*[11]. Quite ambiguously for

---

9 85/374/EC

10 s3(1)

11 s1(2)(c)

our purposes the Act is not clear as to whether software and/or other products of an intellectual type are included in the definition of its scope. Disembodied software per se is typically not treated as a "good" under English law although there is an argument which might encompass software embedded into functional hardware. Anecdotally, the Consumer Rights Act may also provide some correlative instruction so far as Sale of Goods legislation is concerned in its Chapter 3, which explicitly provides that the supply of digital content should be treated neither as goods nor as a service but as a separate class of supply[12]. Chapter eight of this book (Sector Specific Considerations) looks at the implications of Chapter 3 of the CRA in a little more detail.

Finally, there is also the "*developmental risks defence*", which provides a defence to the manufacturer "*if the scientific and technical knowledge at the time the product was manufactured was not such that a producer of a similar product might have been able to discover the defect*"[13]. This is obviously highly relevant to our current discussion – products including machine learning and artificial intelligence will inevitably involve the "state of the art" in relation to their development.

Future Liability Frameworks

Insurance

There are clear public policy arguments now for the introduction of a strict liability insurance-based model for artificially intelligent systems. The 1973 Accident Compensation Act in New Zealand is a classic example of such a system working in practice – it applies generally to compensation for allaccidents. In New Zealand, accidents are not litigated, but rather victim compensation is automatically paid at Government set tariffs and funded by insurance premiums.

---

12 s33 et seq

13 s4(1)e

Negligence and breach of contract actions are becoming more and more complex to litigate – as resources are spent identifying what has (or indeed might) have gone wrong. In particular, the argument runs that from a social justice perspective, it is better spending the money compensating the victims of accidents and incidents involving autonomous systems than it is on expensive lawyers and expert witnesses.

So far as research and development is concerned, a strict liability insurance-based model would also incentivise research on new intelligent AI based systems, rather than forcing R&D divisions of corporations to consider what defensive steps they should be taking to avoid a class action.

What has the UK been doing to address this challenge? We've seen the most movement in the CAV space.

The UK Government recently concluded its consultation document on driverless vehicle development – including an assessment of the way in which such autonomous vehicles should be covered by insurance. This was the snappily titled *"Pathway to Driverless Cars: Proposals to support advanced driver assistance systems and automated vehicle technologies"*[14] which ultimately led to the *Autonomous and Electric Vehicles Bill*, announced in the 2017 Queen's Speech.

So what are the legislative proposals? Rather than go down the strict liability route I mentioned earlier, the government has chosen to address the issue of driverless cars from the perspective of gaps in current insurance coverage caused by fully autonomous driving.

Section 2 of the *Autonomous and Electric Vehicles Bill* as drafted provided that *"where…an accident is caused by an automated vehicle when driving itself…the vehicle is insured at the time of the accident, and…an insured person or any other person suffers damage as a result of the accident, the insurer is liable for that damage."*

---

14 See the government response to the consultation at http://bit.ly/2iLd23x

In essence the principle enshrined in the bill is that if you are hit by an insured party's vehicle that is self-driving at the time, the insurer "at fault" pays out. If you have comprehensive cover then you will also be insured for your own injuries. If the vehicle at fault is not covered by insurance then the Motor Insurers Bureau will pay out in the usual way and seek to recover its losses from the owner of the uninsured vehicle.

This is an essentially pragmatic response that will probably work in an environment where there is a mixed demographic of driverless cars and human piloted ones – it also avoids systemic change to the insurance industry. It does however completely sidestep the causation issues described earlier in this chapter. Crucially, the proposed measure relies very heavily on the ability of insurers to subrogate and therefore bring claims of their own against other third parties, including manufacturers. This will of course be hugely problematic for insurers if the relevant fault or defect cannot easily be traced.

Turing Registries

Some commentators[15] have argued specifically that for intelligent machines we need to go a step further and set up what have been termed "Turing Registries" after the great computer pioneer Alan Turing.

This would work by submitting intelligent machines to a testing and certification process to quantify the certification based on a spectrum as follows: the higher the intelligence and autonomy and hence greater consequences for failure, the higher the premium payable to "release" that machine into the working environment. The premium payable for certification would be paid by the developer or manufacturer of the AI entity wanting to deploy the AI into the market. Much as in the manner of the New Zealand strict liability insurance model discussed earlier, the premiums would fund a "common pool" under which risks

---

15 See for example *"Liability for Distributed Artificial Intelligences"*, Curtis E.A. Karnow, Berkeley Technology Law Journal 1996, Vol 11.1, page 147

would be paid out. The system could become self-fulfilling if AIs were prohibited from use without this certification.

As has been pointed out, this model is similar, but *not identical* to insurance – it does remove causation and proximate cause but also allows for the wilful acts of AIs – normally something that is excluded by insurance.

Individuation or Artificial Personhood

We have already hopefully dispelled the myth that AGI or artificial general intelligence is a close prospect. It is however worth considering briefly the inevitable question of how our liability rules will cope with machines if at some stage they do *individuate* – or develop distinct legal personalities and individual identities of their own. Clearly if machines possess a human equivalent personality of their own then there is no reason why they cannot directly accrue liability through the concept of "*artificial personhood*" in the same manner in which living breathing humans accrue it. The European Parliament considered this question in a recommendation on granting robots and AI's legal status to the Commission on *Civil Law Rules on Robotics*[16]. Part of their recommended approach was to propose a registration system for intelligent robots in much the same manner as the Turing Registries we describe above. The recommendation on special legal personality was recently strongly criticised in an open letter to the Commission signed by over 150 AI and robotics specialists – so it is clear that any further developments in this space are likely to be controversial and hotly contested.

There are no answers here obviously, but rather questions. We can however consider some current and historical legal analogues. How are we going to treat self-aware machines and are we going to fall into the unfortunate historical bear traps of the past? The historical treatment of slaves bears particular scrutiny in this regard and the questions raised by

---

16 27th January 2017 2015/2103 (INL), see in particular paragraph 59 f.

that treatment are no less relevant now, although not for discussion in this book.

If we walk further down the path of individuation, and give them personal liability, how are we going to apply legal duties of care to intelligent machines?

Obviously the law already recognises circumstances where there is a reduced level of legal liability owing to a commensurately reduced ability to distinguish right from wrong – the principle of **Doli Incapax** in relation to infants and the mentally incapable spring to mind in this regard. Might some machines that are not fully capable of understanding the consequences of their actions fall within this principle in the future?

We are now effectively at a "*tipping point*" in how we manage the machine generated consequences of our new AI creations. As we have seen, Contract, Tort and Strict Liability consumer protection laws are effective to a degree in relation to managing these consequences but effectively break down where cause and effect cannot be made out.

CHAPTER THREE
BIG DATA AND ARTIFICIAL INTELLIGENCE

It is of course, big data that sits at the heart of artificial intelligence.

As computing systems generally have grown in power and capacity, so the consumption of data has grown exponentially.

One of the most exciting developments of machine learning is its ability to analyse data in vastly more dimensions than human beings have ever been able to, at a far quicker pace. This ability to spot unexpected correlations and patterns in data is incredibly powerful and has already provided some very surprising applications – one US insurance start up[1] for example can analyse a "selfie" using thousands of different facial data points to determine how quickly an individual is ageing, their gender, body mass index and whether they smoke. Their system predicts life expectancy of individuals much more accurately than traditional methods. Another system developed by researchers at Stanford University can apparently (and somewhat controversially) identify an individual's sexuality by identifying or correlating a complex series of facial characteristics[2].

Not unsurprisingly, the potential for such AI solutions to have a significant impact on personal life and privacy has drawn the attention of legislators and is a feature of the new General Data Protection Regulation (**or "GDPR"**) which we'll look at shortly. Before we do this however, and in order to provide a framework for our analysis, it is worth describing how machine learning systems acquire and generate data and typically how they process such data.

---

1 Lapetus Solutions Inc.

2 https://osf.io/zn79k/ "Deep Neural Networks are more accurate than humans in detecting sexual orientation from facial images", Wang, Kosinski, 2017

It should also be pointed out that the data acquisition and manipulation features of AI systems are not unique to this technology but are amplified to an extreme degree by machine learning. Analytics are very much a product of the complex data producing society that we now live in.

For the most part we tend to think of the handing over of data (including personal data) to third parties as a conscious transaction which we positively have to provide our pro-active consent for. In fact, this is an outmoded view of reality. In many cases now, data (some of which will inevitably be "personal") is generated automatically by the variety of "smart" devices we interact with. Indeed, we don't even need to actively interact with a device for data to be generated about us. We could be the subjects of a facial recognition system at an airport or have our mobile phones queried by MAC "sniffers" without even being aware of it.

Predictive Analytics

The Information Accountability Foundation (IAF) has identified four types of data that form the basis of data analytics[3] – that is to say multiple items of data which in broad terms together disclose a *pattern* (ie typically of usage or consumption in terms of a particular device or movement in terms of surveillance etc.). These types of data are "**Provided**" data (as described above) the most traditional means – that data that is consciously given by individuals. "**Observed**" data might be data drawn from surveillance systems. "**Derived**" data is data drawn directly from other sources to produce new classes of data, and "**Inferred**" data is produced typically by analysis of existing data to make predictions. It is this last class of data which are referred to as predictive data analytics (or more simply *predictive analytics*) where machine learning systems have been making ever impressive technological advances.

---

3 "The origins of personal data and its implications for governance", OECD March 2014

The most immediate influence of this is best illustrated by the systemic impact predictive analytics are having on the insurance industry. Quite apart from the potential jobs impact in relation to claims handling and processing, the technology is transforming the way in which insurance companies model risk and hence price premiums.

At its most simple level, insurers model risk by way of a concept known as "*pooling*". Insurers put large groups of similar people together, using common risk modelling points, and their premiums are used to fund a "common pool". In any given year, some will need to be paid out and some will not. As long as the common pool remains liquid – the system continues to work. Insurance based predictive analytics function by giving insurers more detail about individuals and associated risks. This allows for far more accurate risk pricing and removes the need to pool broad groups of people together.

Obviously this gives rise to a whole host of ethical questions about the availability and pricing of insurance as the technology leads us down the path of what has been referred to as "micro" pooling of insurance risk.

Car driving behaviours are one obvious example which could lead to "risky" behaviours driving up insurance pricing and "safe" behaviours lowering it. Even more serious is the impact of advanced analytics on genetic data which might model susceptibility to genetic disease and therefore impact the pricing and availability of life insurance coverage.

Data Acquisition (or streaming)

Aside from predictive analytics, machine learning systems have a prodigious capacity to self-generate and collect or "smart stream" data whilst they are being used (indeed, some devices, such as autonomous and semi-autonomous vehicles) are pro-actively designed on this basis. What the IAF neglects to include in its analysis is also the category of "**Generated**" data, although this might arguably fall within their category of "Observed" data.

"Smart streaming" of data has already drawn the significant attention of regulators. The European Commission has recently published its *Strategy on Co-Operative Intelligent Transport Systems or "CIT-S"*[4] which sets out its approach to developing a standardised intelligent transport infrastructure allowing vehicles to communicate with each other, with centralised traffic management systems and other highway users. The potential for such data to be misused is clearly troubling – for example not only could a CAV identify a journey destination, it could also potentially also report back on driving habits (when not in autonomous mode) and theoretically identify any traffic offences.

In the context of our discussion such data could obviously also have an impact on the manner in which insurance is offered to the user of the vehicle when under human control.

The policy adopted by the EU Commission has been to identify such data as personal data and therefore afford it the protection of the European data protection framework.

Understanding how AI systems Process Data

We tend to think of traditional computer data processing as the assimilation of large amounts of data which are then varied/changed/updated or adapted in some mechanistic way to support the application or program being utilised by the system.

In contrast, as I indicated in the introduction to this book and at the start of this particular chapter, the inherent value in most AI systems is in their ability to spot patterns, correlations and different dimensionalities in the data sets which they observe. Whilst this may not have a hugely practical consequence so far as the regulatory definitions of "*per-*

---

4 See:
   http://ec.europa.eu/energy/sites/ener/files/documents/1_en_act_part1_v5.pdf

sonal data"[5] and "*processing*"[6] are concerned, it is conceptually important to understand this difference and it is a topic we will return to in the context of intellectual property and artificial intelligence later on in this book.

AI systems tend to observe, learn and model from the large data sets they are exposed to. The value in the utility of such systems is not therefore just in the sense that they can process the data elements in large data sets – it is also in their ability to spot and correlate patterns in such data and learn (or optimise output) through use of the *Learner* element of the system.

The closest analogy is of course a human being learning a new skill. A human will assimilate a skill from tangible materials (data) and training. Irrespective of whether those tangible materials (ie. the data elements) are returned to a third party, lost or subsequently destroyed, the skill and knowhow (or *learned* behaviours) still remain with the person.

The General Data Protection Regulation ("GDPR")

The GDPR ushers in a new era of responsibilities for those who control or process the personal data of EU citizens, and rights for those who are the subjects of such processing. Unfortunately, in pursuing the undoubtedly noble cause of protecting individual citizens the measure, as we shall see in a moment, also creates significant difficulties for the implementers users and owners of artificially intelligent systems – creating a "*Gordian knot*" of regulatory hurdles which often seem to be completely at odds with the practical implications (and business case benefits) of using such systems.

I do not propose in this section to provide a comprehensive guide to the measure which is far reaching beyond the confines of the immediate subject matter – but rather provide a view as to the issues which you

---

5 Article 4(1) GDPR

6 Article 4(2) GDPR

will need to be aware of from a practical and conceptual basis when looking at AI systems that are designed to process personal data.

It goes without saying that machine learning systems which do not process personal data are outside the scope of the legislation – however it pays to remember that personal data is not confined merely to data which refers *directly* or *overtly* to a living individual – the definition is wide enough to encompass data which could achieve such status through a process of *indirect* inference or derivation (see my previous comments under the heading of predictive analytics).

Key Concepts

Before we examine the impact of the GDPR on the users, implementers and owners of artificially intelligent computer systems, it is worth stepping through a few of the concepts which will define our debate. As before, this section will be necessarily led by the focus of this book – that is to say issues within the new EU regulation which are created or caused by artificial intelligence technologies.

"Fair" processing

At its heart, the GDPR mandates that all personal data should be processed *fairly*. Article 5(1)(a) provides that personal data must be *"processed fairly, lawfully and in a transparent manner in relation to the data subject."* As we have seen previously, it is the inherent complexity and "black box" nature of many AI system structures and architectures that causes considerable difficulties in the context of liability and causation. The position is no different in the context of data protection.

At its heart, the concept of fairness is driven by compliance with the Data Protection Principles[7] (which are largely unchanged from the prior

---

7   Article 5 (1) GDPR

regime under the Data Protection Directive) including the concept of transparency.

Transparency is a theme which runs through this narrative and in this context self-evidently refers to the manner in which the processing is publicised and clear to the data subject. This requirement generally refers to the purposes for which personal data are to be utilised, but as we shall see in a little more detail later, it *also* refers to the way in which such data is *computationally* processed by the AI system.

Generally speaking, the requirement of transparency is achieved procedurally under the GDPR by reference to the provision of *"fair processing"* or privacy information notices to the affected data subjects stating (*inter alia*) who the relevant parties are who will be controlling and processing their information, for what purposes it will be processed and who such data is going to be shared with. This however is but the starting point for such notices. There are significant practical and procedural difficulties applying this process to machine learning technologies, particularly given that the GDPR is much more prescriptive about how such notices should be designed and what they should (and should not) achieve, more of which we discuss below.

Consent vs. Legitimate Interests

The lawfulness or otherwise of the relevant processing is also central to the regulatory framework. For the purposes of this debate, this will largely be driven by two of the concepts listed in Article 6 of the GDPR – either that *"the data subject has given consent to the processing of his or her personal data"*[8] or the *"processing is necessary for the purposes of the legitimate interests pursued by the controller... except where such interests are overridden by the interests or fundamental rights and freedoms of the data subject which require protection of personal data..."*

---

8   Article 6(1)a

Under the data protection regime prior to the introduction of the GDPR, consent of the data subject had become somewhat of a discredited concept – many businesses had adopted the approach of burying general consent deep in a raft of obscure terms and conditions, or pre-populating check boxes, forcing data subjects to proactively "uncheck" in order *not* to give consent. Again, European legislators have effectively blocked these practices under the GDPR and strengthen the concept, stating that *"...Consent should be given by a clear affirmative act establishing a freely given specific, informed and unambiguous indication of the data subject's agreement as to the processing of personal data...this could include...conduct which clearly indicates in this context the data subject's acceptance of the proposed processing of his personal data. Silence, pre-ticked boxes or inactivity should not therefore constitute consent."*[9]. The natural corollary of this of course is that the individual data subject is free to withdraw such consent at any time – indeed this is the position that is legislated for in Article 7(3) of the GDPR.

For the purposes of our current analysis, and indeed generally in relation to all personal data processing based on this ground, it does of course mean that consent as a lawful basis for processing has been dramatically reduced in utility – on any objective basis, why go to the trouble of obtaining pro-active consent for processing in relation to a particular purpose – including significant levels of investment in systems and technology to carry out such activity if consent can be withdrawn at any time by any individual ?

This practical problem with pro-active consent has meant that may businesses are now seeking to rely on *legitimate interests* instead. It is this sea change in approach which is fuelling a healthy growth in GDPR audit assessment activity – because simply put, if a business seeks to rely on their *legitimate interests* as a lawful ground, they must undertake a comprehensive and detailed assessment which balances these interests with the rights and interests of the data subjects concerned. The point here is that the processing must be *necessary* for the data controller's legitimate interests, and not merely *convenient*. Article 13(1)d of the

---

9 See Recital 32 of the GDPR

GDPR provides that where a data controller is relying on the legitimate interests ground, it must explain this in the relevant privacy information notice.

Profiling

Article 4(4) of the GDPR introduces the concept of *"profiling"* which will be of particular relevance to the use of AI systems evaluating and making decisions on data sets comprised of large amounts of personal data. This provides that profiling means *"any form of automated processing of personal data consisting of the use of personal data to evaluate certain aspects relating to a natural person, in particular to analyse or predict aspects concerning that natural person's performance at work, economic situation, health, personal preferences, interests, reliability, behaviour, location or movements"*.

The three key aspects of the profiling process are that it should be automated; carried out using personal data and utilised to evaluate personal aspects of a natural person. It is clear that the legislators intended this concept to be construed as widely as possible[10], so that whilst the decision making involved has to include some form of automated processing, it does not rule out human intervention per se. Equally speaking, profiling does not need to involve the higher predictive elements of a machine learning system – it can e.g. simply entail the classification of people in terms of their gender, race and interests.

---

10 See the Article 29 Working Party paper entitled "Guidelines on Automated individual decision making and Profiling for the purposes of Regulation 2016/679 (3 October 2017)

Automated Decision Making

Article 22(1) introduces another key concept, that of automated decision making. This may or may not include profiling but is distinguished from the former as being performed solely by machine (ie with no human intervention).

The GDPR includes a right for data subjects *"not to be subject to a decision which is based solely on automated processing, including profiling, which produces legal effects concerning him or her or similarly significantly affects him or her."* What this provision significantly creates is a prohibition on such automated decisions unless the exceptions in the rest of the article are satisfied. For completeness, these are where the decision is necessary for the purposes of entering into a contract[11]; is authorised by EU or member state law[12] or based on the explicit consent of the data subject[13].

The concern of the legislators here is to protect data subjects from being prejudiced by automated decisions which will fundamentally affect them, such as for example being refused credit or a mortgage. Remember also that this analysis should not necessarily be confined solely to "*obtained*" data – it could also apply to data that has been "*derived*" or "*inferred*" – that is to say correlated indirectly without being proactively handed over by the data subject concerned.

In the world of big data this is a substantial concern for those businesses that work on a large scale. Artificially intelligent systems have the ability to substantially increase processing speed whilst retaining sophistication in the assessments applied to such decisions. Without commenting on the socio-political and ethical aspects of such an approach, this is an undoubted technological advantage for those citizens who ultimately benefit and for whom the outcome would otherwise be delayed. This

---

11 Article 22(2)a

12 Article 22(2)b

13 Article 22(2)c

"unsupervised" model is now effectively constrained throughout the European member states. EU law mandates that there needs to be some form of *meaningful* human intervention in the process. As the Article 29 Working Party states "*the controller cannot avoid the Article 22 provisions by fabricating human involvement*".

Another highly problematic area for machine learning, which is likely to include significant degrees of automated decision making, is that the *legitimate interests* lawful ground is not available when processing such data in these circumstances – we have already discussed the practical concerns and limitations stemming from use of *consent* as a lawful ground.

Purpose limitation and data minimisation

The concepts covered by Articles 5(1)(b) and 5(1)(c) of the GDPR, which continue with the so called "*purpose limitation*" and "*data minimisation*" principles are also potential hurdles to the implementation of certain classes of machine learning systems. They explicitly provide that personal data should be "*collected for specified and legitimate purpose and not further processed in a manner which is incompatible with those purposes*" and it should also be "*adequate, relevant and limited to what is necessary in relation to the purposes for which they are processed*".

As we discussed earlier, it is self-evident that these requirements *could* potentially impede the use of unsupervised machine learning (the so called Rumsfeldian "*unknown knowns*") in a big data context. Such systems generate potentially useful analysis or correlation of data sets in circumstance that could not reasonably have been predicted or anticipated at the outset (such as the example quoted at the beginning of this chapter in relation to facial characteristics leading to a correlation in sexuality).

Privacy by Design

The final concept that is worth discussing in this section is that of *"privacy by design"*. This approach, which is mandated by the GDPR[14], was not a requirement of the prior Data Protection Directive. Encouragingly, it is this principle which may assist the users and owners of machine learning systems that have a personal data impact.

What privacy by design (technically *"privacy by design and privacy by default"*) requires is a structured design approach when creating a new information processing system which enshrines the concept of data privacy at its heart, rather than bolting it on as an afterthought which is so often the case in system architecture design. This entails a root and branch analysis of the operational and ethical reasons why the personal data are needed and a full understanding of the impact of such data collection on the potential data subjects. The Privacy Commissioner of Ontario in Canada has published what is widely regarded as the leading conceptual approach in achieving privacy by design, by setting out seven foundational principles which should be at the heart of any such approach[15].

A first step on the path towards achieving privacy by design is by use of what are known as Privacy Impact Assessments (or PIAs) (which are not to be confused with Privacy information notices). Article 35 of the GDPR provides that *"Where a type of processing in particular using new technologies, and taking into account the nature, scope, context and purposes of the processing, is likely to result in a high risk to the rights and freedoms of natural persons, the Controller shall, prior to the processing,*

---

14 Article 25 GDPR

15 See Privacy by Design, A Primer by the Ontario Privacy Commissioner. Broadly speaking the seven principles accord with the general approach outlined above – by defining e.g. a proactive, not a reactive approach, making privacy a default setting, embedding privacy into the solution design, applying a positive sum (not a zero sum) approach, providing for full lifecycle protection, keeping use of fata visible and transparent and ensuring respect for user privacy.

carry out an assessment of the impact of the envisaged processing operations on the protection of personal data."[16]

Understanding information flows – what is collected and when, how it stored and for what purposes and how such data is computationally processed through the relevant system are a key part of such analysis. As we have previously discussed, any difficulties in explaining the computational processes of a *"black box"* AI system will therefore need to be balanced very carefully with cogent, ethical and logical reasons for such collection and processing, which can significantly justify the benefits of using such a system for the relevant data processing application.

Privacy information notices

All of this brings us back to the GDPR requirement that we discussed at the beginning of this chapter of ensuring *transparency* in processing by use of privacy information or "*fair processing*" notices.

As you will recall, these are required whether a business is seeking to rely on the legitimate interests or consent ground for lawful processing. Whilst admirable as a concept, such notices have the potential to create substantial difficulties in the context of artificial intelligence and machine learning, especially bearing in mind the complexity and *"black box"* nature of such systems.

Articles 12, 13 and 14 of the GDPR provide a particularly clear example of the potentially irreconcilable tautologies involved, by stipulating on the one hand that such notices should be "...*concise, transparent, intelligible and easily accessible...using clear and plain language...*"[17] whilst on the other hand stating that where automated decision making and/or profiling is involved that "...*meaningful information about the logic involved...*"[18] is also supplied. This is evidently not an easy tightrope to negotiate – particularly in a machine learning

---

16 Article 35(1) GDPR

17 Article 12(1) GDPR

context. The logical first approach might be to provide a detailed explanation for the data subject setting out the context and grounds for the processing and explaining in detail the computational details of the AI system being used, however this is likely to have the opposite effect of confusing the data subject or overloading them with information. Indeed, the Article 29 Working Party has specifically stated that "*information fatigue*" should be avoided[19].

With perhaps a nod to this tautology, the framers of the legislation have indicated that there are various mechanisms which can be used to highlight in a user-friendly way, the information which is required to be conveyed to the users of such systems.

The first accessible method which could be used is to implement clear iconography (on the basis that a picture is worth a thousand words) into the relevant privacy information notice. The use of icons is not a new approach, however the key has been to develop a consistent set of symbols which have an apparent individual meaning and read consistently with each other – often easier said than done. The GDPR provides a mechanism for the introduction of standardised icons under Article 12(8), but as yet there are no agreed forms.

The second method is very much context driven and depends upon the nature of the system involved and the manner in which personal data are to be collected – it is however of relevance to complex information processing systems and relies on making relevant information available to the data subject when it is needed, rather than in one large undigestible notice up front. "*Just in time*" notices as they a referred to rely on statements on information processing being given at the time a relevant question is being asked of an individual (through the use e.g. of pop-up or pop-over dialogue boxes). These can be coupled with an approach with allows for "*layering*" – basic information being made available with a "*click through*" link for those users who desire to have

---

18 Articles 13(2)(f) and 14(2)(g) GDPR

19 See Paragraph 7 of the Article 29 Working Party paper on Transparency 17/EN
   WP260

access to more detailed information about the manner in which their data will be processed.

It does not take a lot of imagination to see that innovative adoption of these techniques (which whilst potentially difficult to conceptualise at the outset), may provide implementers of machine learning systems with a route through the potentially conflicting requirements of Articles 12, 13 & 14 of the GDPR.

The Data Protection Act 2018

The UK's forthcoming separation from the European Union, or Brexit as it has commonly become known, adds unfortunately another degree of complexity to what is an undoubtedly a difficult legislative context to navigate for the users of machine learning systems. The new Data Protection Act, which was enacted into law synchronously with the General Data Protection Regulation on May 25th 2018, aims to enshrine the essential principles of the GDPR into UK law post-Brexit.

Unfortunately, in the legislators' assiduous attempts to "*gold plate*" the UK's data protection compliance (no doubt fostered by a desire to attain equivalence with the remaining member states of the EU in terms of data transfers), the measure includes some criminal sanctions for companies and somewhat more worryingly, personal criminal sanctions for company directors. Whilst the Act does not provide for custodial sentences on breach (the sanctions are in essence limited to fines), these new offences will no doubt add a degree of real anxiety, given the irreconcilable tautologies in the GDPR we have discussed above, to those who seek to use and implement machine learning solutions post-Brexit.

It is worthwhile considering two in particular that have been introduced in relation to personal data and understanding their potential implications for artificial intelligence.

Unlawful obtaining of personal data

The Act provides in section 170 that *"it is an offence for a person knowingly or recklessly (a) to obtain or disclose personal data without the consent of the controller, (b) to procure the disclosure of personal data to another person without the consent of the controller, or (c) after obtaining personal data, to retain it without the consent of the person who was the controller in relation to the personal data when it was obtained."*[20]. Sub-sections (1) and (2) provide for various defences, including in relation to the prevention or detection of crime; for the purposes of law or court order; and justified disclosure in the public interest. It is also a defence if you can show that the controller would have consented had they known or if you had a reasonable (if incorrect) belief that you were authorised to disclose. This offence is similar to the one in the previous 1998 Data Protection Act – however it is extended to include the retention of personal data. As we discuss in the context of intellectual property in Chapter four (see under the paragraph headed "*The learned behaviours paradigm*"), there is a tendency of machine learning systems to retain what I have described as "*information residuals*" – principally the associative and correlative aspects describing statistical patterns and correlations in data used by the system (rather than the content of that data itself) – being retained by the machine learning system in an analogous fashion to a taught human being. The simple anthropomorphic analogy is that once something is learned, it cannot be unlearned. Clearly personal data processed by machine learning systems can be returned once it has been used – the question is whether what remains – the *information residuals* – constitutes retention for the purposes of this offence.

Re-identification of de-identified personal data

Section 171 creates an offence of re-identification of de-identified personal data: *"(1) It is an offence for a person knowingly or recklessly to re-identify information that is de-identified personal data without the consent*

---

20 Section 170(1) of the Data Protection Act 2018

of the controller responsible for de-identifying the personal data. ... (a) personal data is "de-identified" if it has been processed in such a manner that it can no longer be attributed, without more, to a specific data subject; (b) a person "re-identifies" information if the person takes steps which result in the information no longer being de-identified within the meaning of paragraph (a)"[21]. This offence is aimed at protecting data which has been *pseudonymised* (where re-identification is possible) (as opposed to fully anonymised where it should be impossible to re-identify data subjects). Users of machine learning systems should be mindful of the powerful ability of such systems to apply predictive analytics to the data that they process (see earlier in this chapter under the heading *"Predictive Analytics"*). In the context of our immediate debate the risk must be to prevent or at least put in place measures to avoid a machine learning system from *deriving* or *inferring* sufficient characteristics in the data it processes to inadvertently re-identify data subjects.

---

21 Section 171(1) & (2) of the Data Protection Act 2018

CHAPTER FOUR
INTELLECTUAL PROPERTY
RIGHTS IN AI SYSTEMS

Traditionally intellectual property (or "*IP*") concepts form part of our established methods of protection for new technologies. In this chapter, we'll take a look at how IP can and cannot be used to protect investment and innovation in the development of artificial intelligence. We'll also consider whether intellectual property conventions, as in the context of causation earlier, may be breaking down, or at least fraying at the edges.

Before we examine some of the IP frameworks which might be applicable to machine learning, it is worthwhile taking some time to assess where the perceived *inherent value* in such technology lies, because in simple terms, if we can defend the valuable elements, we are more effectively protecting our entire AI asset. These considerations are clearly not only important from the perspective of the users and licensors of such technology, but also those who wish to obtain such systems through corporate activity (such as mergers and acquisitions).

As we learned in Chapter one, AI systems are not radically different from traditional computer systems in that they are essentially composed of two elements – the software which embodies the relevant AI model, and the computational hardware upon which it sits. Of course computational systems that host complex deep learning AI models are very sophisticated and can access huge amounts of processing power as well as harnessing petabytes of data – but they are still computers in the conventional sense.

At a superficial level one might say therefore that nothing has changed from an IP perspective, and that these are trite and settled issues: the computational hardware per se or in combination with software might in theory be eligible for patent protection under the Patents Act 1977, but that would require the elements of that Act to be made out – principally the element of industrial application[1] which requires a physical device or apparatus together with newness and an *inventive step* taking the physical device beyond the published *state of the art*[2].

Disembodied software does not (at least within the EU and UK) qualify for patent protection[3] – here we must look to the Copyright, Designs and Patents Act 1988 (the "CDPA") which specifically calls out human and machine generated software as capable of protection by copyright[4] provided it meets the required standards of originality. However, it is here that we see some of the logic underpinning software as copyrightable works beginning to break down.

Whilst the CDPA does make provision for computer generated works to be protected by Copyright[5], this still presumes a causal connection (albeit vague) between the relevant acts of the computer and human preparatory work – section 9(3) provides that "*In the case of a literary, dramatic, musical or artistic work which is computer-generated, the author shall be taken to be the person by whom the arrangements necessary for the creation of the work are undertaken.*". The term "*Computer generated*" is defined as follows "*in relation to a work, means that the work is generated by computer in circumstances such that there is no human author of the work.*"[6]. As we have seen, and as I explain further below, machine learning models are increasingly abstracted from human intervention

---

1 See s1(1)(c) Patents Act 1977

2 See s1(1)(b) Patents Act 1977

3 s1(2)(c) Patents Act 1977 excludes specifically "a scheme, rule or method for performing a mental act, playing a game or doing business, or a program for a computer"

4 s3(1)(b) Copyright, Designs and Patents Act 1977 specifically includes computer programs as literary works and s12(7) makes explicit provision for works that are generated by Computer, reducing the applicable copyright term to 50 years from the end of the calendar year in which the work was created.

5 S9(3) Copyright, Designs and Patents Act 1988

6 S178 Copyright, Designs and Patents Act 1988

and inherently opaque, and thus, it is argued, the causal connection implied by section 9(3) is becoming increasingly redundant. Indeed the one UK case that has to date been decided in relation to computer generated works – *Nova Productions ltd v. Mazooma Games*[7] applying section 9(3) of the CDPA, provides a highly problematic outcome for the "*learned behaviours*" paradigm I discuss below. Mazooma held that a series of computer generated video game "frames" were either authored directly by the machine or by the person providing arrangements necessary for the creation of the work – in this case, the programmer – and not the *player* of the game. In our current debate, is it not the *trainer* of the machine learning system which is most analogous to the *player*?

As we discovered in Chapter one, the key elements forming a machine learning system are the **Model**, the **Parameters** and the **Learner** which together form the Artificial Neural Network. The CDPA provides that a literary work "*means any work, other than a dramatic or musical work, which is written, spoken or sung, and accordingly includes...(b) a computer program*" and "*(c) preparatory design material for a computer program*"[8]. It would seem evident in this context that at least the AI **Model** (the logical framework within which the system operates) described above will potentially be eligible for copyright protection. Whilst the CDPA provides no guidance as to originality required for such protection, recital eight of the 2009 Software Directive[9] provides that in determining whether "*a computer program is an original work, no tests as to the qualitative or aesthetic merits of the program should be applied.*" This is to be read in conjunction with Article 1 which provides that "*a computer program shall be protected if it is original in the sense that it is the author's own intellectual creation. No other criteria shall be applied to determine its eligibility for protection.*"[10] Clearly the framers of the Directive intended copyright protection to extend merely to the coding aspects of the

7   [2007] EWCA Civ 219, [2007] Bus LR 1032

8   s(3)(1) of the Copyright, Designs and Patents Act 1977

9   Directive 2009/24/EC on the legal protection of computer programs

10 See Article 1(3), Directive 2009/24/EC

software concerned and in turn expressly excluded the *outputs* or *products* of that code. Whilst there is no such guidance in the UK CDPA, the Directive should be considered as influential on the approach taken by courts and tribunals within the European Member States.

Obviously at the time the relevant Copyright legislation was framed, software (whether machine or human created) consisted of rigidly programmed linear instruction sets that have no (or at least very limited) ability to adapt and "learn" according to data inputs: the exponential rise in use and development of artificial intelligence has occurred relatively recently.

As we have seen, machine learning systems lack a direct correlation between human input and machine generated output – their models are created within the framework of software but as they are trained or exposed to sufficient amounts of data, their outputs adapt (they are modified by the *Learner* element we discussed in Chapter one, above), and thus they become more adept at solving the application that they are presented with. Machine learning trainers are therefore in a highly influential position to tune and direct system outputs (in this regard I direct the reader back to comments made at the beginning of this chapter in relation to the *Mazooma* case).

It is this complex mass of tuned, biased and weighted variables applied progressively to the machine learning model during the training process – in more anthropomorphic terms – *"learned"* or *"trained"* behaviour (discussed further below) – which provides the key difference and arguably the demonstrable and substantial *value* to the users of AI systems. Other than this distinguishing feature there is no underlying difference in the technological hardware and processing platform as between trained and untrained systems. Of course, continuing the anthropomorphic analogy, which is entirely apposite here, the other aspect of learned behaviours is that once they are learned, they cannot be unlearned, and the more relevant learning and experience you are exposed to, the better you get at solving a particular problem. This is of particular importance in relation to the large data sets that AI systems are exposed to, especially in circumstances where such data sets are *licensed* for use (implying some form of return of the material so licensed) rather than assigned permanently or owned by the user. We'll consider these two elements of what I have termed the *learned behaviours paradigm* in a moment.

Separately, and distinct from the system itself, there is clearly value in the training data sets that are provided to the relevant machine learning system. This is akin of course to the training materials provided to a child in school education – feed it the right information and hopefully the right outputs will emerge (the child will be properly educated). Don't feed it at all, or feed it the wrong information and what you'll get out of it will also be a waste of time – as the saying goes, "*garbage in, garbage out*". Curating and assembling training data sets (whether on a supervised or unsupervised basis) is, as we have already mentioned, a critical part in the evolution and development of a useful artificially intelligent system. One has to assume that there will therefore be some not inconsiderable level of skill involved in creating such data sets, and calibrating them to ensure maximal value from a machine learning system.

Algorithms

Algorithms sit at the heart of artificially intelligent systems – clearly the efficiency or otherwise of such algorithms drives the usefulness of such systems – however it is important to note that algorithms *per se* are nothing more than a complex procedural expression or set of rules – a formula.

In the case of machine learning systems, it is algorithms which define at the most fundamental level how the system handles and manages the data inputted into it.

Algorithms fall within a grey area in intellectual property law. When they are expressed as pure mathematical formulae, they are unlikely to be capable of copyright protection as they represent an expression of mathematical fact. However when expressed, encoded and articulated as part of software, they are more likely in principle to enjoy copyright protection.

So far as patent law is concerned, obviously an algorithm represents an idea or concept. As such, unless the prior rules we discussed above are followed (principally *industrial application* by embodiment in a physical apparatus, *newness* and *inventive step*), they are unlikely to be patentable. In any event, focussing merely on the protection of the learning or activation algorithms used by an artificially intelligent system (if indeed such are capable of intellectual property protection) solves only one part of the IP jigsaw. An algorithm to a machine learning system is an expression of its most fundamental functions – taking such an approach to the exclusion of the other elements listed in this chapter would be much like attempting to protect the representative chemical synaptic functions of neurons in a human brain whilst excluding its thoughts.

The "learned behaviours" paradigm

Earlier on in this chapter, we described how artificial intelligence systems develop useful learned behaviours over the course of their training process by the refinement of weights, biases and variables within their AI *models* (whether on a supervised, unsupervised or reinforcement basis) and how more comprehensively or effectively trained systems are demonstrably more valuable than their counterparts which although technologically equivalent, have not undergone this process. It is worth recapping the concept of machine learning in order to get a clear picture of what is actually happening inside a machine learning system.

As we saw in Chapter one, what a neural network does when it "*learns*" is apply a series of weights and biases across the successive artificial neuron layers in its network to influence activations within those individual neurons and ultimately the output layer, hopefully achieving the desired correct output. It is ultimately a mathematical process of refinement but a process which leads to optimised and useful output. As noted above, I refer to this for reasons of conceptual ease as "learned behaviour".

We also considered that exposure to training or calibrating sets of data during this training process (and indeed to live production data during normal operational use) could lead to some elements of the data set – principally the associative aspects describing statistical patterns and correlations rather than the content itself – being retained by the machine learning system in an analogous fashion to a taught human being. How then should this paradigm be managed by intellectual property law?

We have seen that copyright will somewhat imperfectly protect the software model or framework within which an artificial intelligence system sits. On the same basis, it might also protect relevant machine learning algorithms but only if they are expressed in a software form. It cannot (in its current guise) protect the output or *learned behaviours* of that system, unless they are expressed in an immutable form in the software construct of the *Model* (as discussed earlier). Immutability however is typically not a characteristic of learned behaviours. As with a human, as a machine learning system is trained and exposed to more data, it becomes better at its assigned task – or in more mechanistic terms, the output becomes further optimised. Patent law in contrast will not protect disembodied software, or algorithms but could in theory protect a physical device with software embedded on it.

Knowhow

Traditionally *"know how"*, that is to say the knowledge and knowhow gained by a person experientially and locked up in their heads, is not something that is capable of intellectual property protection. Typically this is because, in human terms, intellectual property protects the *expressions* of ideas rather than the idea itself. Without delving too deeply into the realms of the philosophical, can it be said that the "knowhow" generated by artificially intelligent systems is equivalent?

In practical terms of course, machine learning systems are created by human beings and (for the moment at least) do not share an equivalence with us. They are undoubtedly complex, and we as humans have difficulty understanding on a practical (and even theoretical level) how such systems reach their decisions, but they are still a construct of human endeavour.

Whilst copyright and patent law are unlikely to be of much use in relation to protecting the learned behaviours of trained artificially intelligent systems, it is submitted that in this context there is one intellectual property route that might be extended to protect them, and that is the so-called "*trade secret*".

A trade secret is typically a commercially valuable process or item of know-how which has been kept from the public domain.

Traditionally the UK has not had a trade secret regime but has relied on the concept of breach of confidence for protection of such items. Whilst this common law regime provides much equivalence with Trade Secret law, it has traditionally suffered from some conceptual difficulties with the concept of industrial espionage. The United States has long had a trade secret law – see for example the Uniform Trade Secrets Act of 1979 and in this context the EU is perceived as having lagged behind in its intellectual property regime. This has led to the recently published *Directive on the Protection of undisclosed know-how and business information (trade secrets)[11]* or Trade Secrets Directive. The Trade Secrets Directive provides that an item of intellectual property will qualify for protection if: it "*(a) it is secret in the sense that it is not, as a body or in the precise configuration and assembly of its components, generally known among or readily accessible to persons within the circles that normally deal with the kind of information in question; (b) it has commercial value because it is secret; (c) it has been subject to reasonable steps under the circumstances, by the person lawfully in control of the information, to keep it secret*".[12] In the context of our current debate, the learned behaviours (or

---

11 Directive (EU) 2016/943

12 Trade Secrets Directive Article 1(a),(b) & (c)

optimised outputs) of an artificially intelligent system are likely to have been developed through a careful process which will be a combination of training, tuning and exposure to carefully selected training data sets (of which more later). Much of this process is likely to have been developed through experimentation, trial and error and of course considerable investment.

It is likely in the circumstances that the "optimised" machine learning system that results will result in competitive advantage for its owner, and such owner is unlikely to want to voluntarily throw that competitive advantage away by disclosing it to competitors.

Provided the owner has exercised reasonable precautions to keep the process described above away from the public domain, it is plausible that they should be able to claim trade secret protection under the regime proposed by the Trade Secrets Directive. The foregoing should of course be tempered by the fact that there is a very strong academic research community that will be driven by "*open access*" principles to information, for the greater good of advancing research into artificial intelligence and there are equally speaking very many open source derived AI algorithms and approaches which obviously will be unlikely to qualify for such intellectual property protection.

Data sets

Custom assembled training data sets (or indeed operational data sets that have been assembled for processing by an AI system) are also, for the reasons articulated above, likely to qualify for similar trade secret style protection.

The informed reader may also wonder about the reach of the Database Directive[13] into this domain – however as that directive is intended to cover a "*scheme of arrangement of data*" (ie a systemically organised

---

13 96/9/EC implemented by the Copyright and Rights in Databases Regulations 1997

database[14]) it is unlikely to be of use in relation to most AI systems whose very power and flexibility comes from their ability to ingest and process multiple items of raw, heterogenous data from different and disparate data sources (sometimes referred to as "data lakes"). Although there are likely to be qualitative decisions made about the types and classes of data to be used for training machine learning systems it is improbable that such data sets would reach the levels of organisation equivalent to a classically ordered database. In the context of neural networks, there may be a role for the Database Directive tangentially in relation to the collective *weights* and *biases* which are applied to individual input neurons in order to influence the network's output (see our earlier discussion on this in the context of Chapter one) – however that analysis appears marginal when one considers that it depends upon these variables being able to be systematically extracted from the operation of the system itself in a useful and repeatable manner.

The second part of the learned behaviours paradigm we discussed above was the potential for an AI system to retain associative and relational elements of the data processed by it as part of the training or learning process – such retention enabling improvement in the system's ability to achieve its assigned tasks or in alternate terms, improving its skill level. Conceptually this is difficult to reconcile with traditional intellectual licensing models and data protection law which require the return or destruction of licensed materials at the end of the applicable licensing term or period of use. Irrespective of whether technically such is feasible, as a developer or owner of a machine learning system you are unlikely to want to hand back those associative or relational data elements (so called *"information residuals"*) which have improved performance in your system. What this means in practical terms is that any licensing model must take account of these characteristics and either provide for a perpetual license of those data elements which are

---

14 Article 1(2) of the Database Directive 96/9/EC provides that "database" means " a collection of independent works, data or other materials arranged in a systematic or methodical way and individually accessible by electronic or other means."

retained or a full assignment. A failure to do so will render the licensee potentially subject to an action for breach of contract.

Whether this proves to be a substantive issue in the future remains to be seen – practically speaking this is the way in which AI systems function so it would seem to be futile attempting to legislate otherwise. As a practitioner however, you should be aware of this pitfall and provide for appropriate carve outs in any third party deals which are licensing data sets for machine learning systems.

Infringing and Derivative works

The final part of this chapter is really to flag the ongoing potential for machine learning systems to create infringing and derivative versions of copyrighted works. This is not of itself a new problem – new technologies have enabled a technologically sophisticated environment which empowers the YouTube generation to manipulate video and audio on domestic computers which has in turn driven a culture of plagiarism and derivative works – a perennial problem for major copyright holders. What is new however, and potentially disturbing, is the level of sophistication that AI provides to these users.

"DeepFake" software, which is now freely available to computer enthusiasts, enables facial substitution technology in video. Inevitably, this has been driven to the lowest common denominator which has involved pasting the faces of Hollywood "A" list actors into hard core pornography (a course of conduct that could of course give rise to wider defamatory issues) – however it doesn't take much imagination to see this technology being used by fans to paste themselves into their favourite franchises, to substitute or swap preferred actors in movies or even to resurrect long dead actors (something that Hollywood is beginning to dabble in on an "official" basis).

In summary we have learned that in the context of artificial intelligence, it is not sufficient to purely rely on the concepts of copyright and patents law – although these still remain fundamentally important, they do not provide one hundred percent coverage and protection for such systems. Trade secret law also has a part to play in protecting investment in machine learning systems that have been taught, tuned and refined through a process of exposure to carefully curated data sets.

So far as the data sets themselves are concerned, you need to ensure (as owner or developer of a machine learning system) that you allow for *information residuals* to be retained by your system. As a licensor of third party data sets to a machine learning system developer, you should consider how this fact is to be reflected commercially and legally in your licences.

CHAPTER FIVE
AUTOMATED BIAS AND DISCRIMINATION

One of the very powerful benefits of artificial intelligence when coupled with big data is the ability of such systems to make predictions or synthesise outputs based on the data which have been presented to them. There is an oft quoted popular fallacy which assumes infallibility and impartiality in such systems – in effect that they are immune from bias.

The partial truth of course is that whilst machines are generally impervious to human emotion when making decisions –as we shall see in this chapter, this does not necessarily equate to lack of subjectivity in such decisions.

AI systems are very dependent on the quality of the data that is fed into them – they need accurate and representative data sets in order to learn and refine their processing of their assigned application – whether that is on a supervised, unsupervised or reinforcement basis.

Being "*fed*" training data and ongoing operational data is critical to performance improvement and enhancement. This is sometimes referred to as the "*data diet vulnerability*".

The data diet vulnerability described above gives rise to another practical legal consideration in relation to the use of machine learning systems – that is the extent to which if such training and operational data sets do contain bias, or are skewed in a particular direction (to e.g. reinforce a specific outcome) they can give rise to automated decisions which are likely to prejudice or discriminate against individuals. In particular it also raises the question of how such bias should be managed at law.

It is an established fact that automating a process – or relegating it to technology can ironically (and somewhat perversely) act to *reduce* oversight in relation to bias thus perpetuating the fallacy of impartiality I describe above.

We are all conditioned to believe in the efficiency of computers. This is clearly a disturbing consideration (and one which should be overtly challenged) where such systems are using data that overtly refers to personally identifiable information. It is especially concerning when one considers that the vulnerability could be deliberately and malevolently exploited in order to make a system biased or discriminatory in addition to the consequences of accidental "*skewing*". Remember also that the breadth of such impact should also be taken into account – consider our earlier discussion on the characteristics of data – discrimination or bias could result from data which indirectly refers to an individual or which is *inferred* or *derived* from other data.

In addition to the problem of training data sets "hard coding" bias into an artificially intelligent system, there is also the problem of the so-called "*filter bubble*" effect – which in reality is an extension of the algorithmic bias described above.

Filter bubble effects occur during operational use of AI systems as they learn and adapt outputs to user behaviour – these can act to reinforce or compound bias by serving up decisions and results which are within the data bubble and excluding those which are outside it – even when in some circumstances, the excluded results may be legitimate.

Typically filter bubbles are discussed in the context of intelligent web browsers that try to direct and focus search results based on previous internet browsing behaviour, but the analysis is equally valid in situations where an AI system has learned (through application of data sets) to select or make choices in a distinct manner.

One example which particularly illustrates these problems is in relation to automated recruitment. The recruitment industry has embraced automation wholeheartedly – especially in relation to those jobs which are perceived as commoditised or where the industry must achieve large scale volume recruitment for clients in short timescales. Sectors where there is high demand for interim employment also find such automated approaches attractive. The net result has been a boom in the development of systems that can automate selection and rejection of CVs, right the way through to chatbots or robotic interviewers that can lead discussions and filter candidates.

Whilst no one doubts the efficiency of such systems when properly implemented, there are concerns that exclusive dependence on them could, aside from the potential for discrimination and bias described above, lead to recruitment which is based purely on documented skills (via CVs) ignoring softer metrics such as an individual's personality, fit and emotional temperament. This is but one example however – there are many instances in modern society where we are increasingly ceding complex decisions which relate to such matters as the finance we can obtain to the news we read to machine learning systems.

The GDPR

So far as the law itself is concerned, it is the General Data Protection Regulation which provides an overarching framework in relation to machine based decisions. The greatest potential impact for individuals is of course is in relation to those decisions that have "*legal affects that significantly affect data subjects*"[1] – and it is in this context and in the context of profiling[2] which the GDPR attempts to address – see the commentary in Chapter three above.

Clearly automated bias and discrimination was one of the problems that the GDPR was implemented to address. We have already discussed the key principles that apply in these circumstances but it is worth covering generally what the GDPR provides for both in terms of punitive sanctions against controllers and processors that breach the provisions of the regulation and individual remedies for EU citizens who have been unfairly discriminated against – or made the subject of bias.

---

1   Article 22 – GDPR

2   Article 4(4) GDPR

The GDPR significantly increases the levels of administrative fines that can be levied on data controllers and expands this punitive regime to data processors for the first time. Clearly the amounts of such fines will depend upon the individual circumstances of the particular case and a number of other factors, such as the seriousness of the breach and the extent to which the breach has been repeated[3] but it is evident that European legislators intended the obligations relating to profiling and automated decision making[4] to be subject to an increased level of sanction – up to the higher of €20m or 4% of the total worldwide annual turnover of an undertaking[5].

We have already seen in Chapter three that data controllers which carry out profiling or automated decision making (as defined by Article 22 of the GDPR) can only do so on the basis of the explicit consent of the data subject[6] and that such consent can be withdrawn at any time. Data subjects have additional rights to rectification[7] – the right to obtain from a data controller without undue delay the rectification of inaccurate personal data relating to them (in addition to the right to have incomplete or partial data on them completed), as well as a right to erasure (the so called *"right to be forgotten"*)[8]. This is all in addition to a right to direct compensation for data subjects which is enshrined in Article 82 of the Regulation.

It is evident there are a comprehensive suite of remedies and sanctions that are available to counter potential bias and discrimination in relation to processing under the GDPR. However there remains a major

---

3 See Article 83(2)(a)-(k) GDPR for a complete list of qualifying factors

4 Article 22 GDPR

5 Article 83(5)(b) GDPR

6 Article 22(2)(a)-(b) provide for additional carve outs related to the performance of contract obligations and specific authorisations of a Member State, see earlier Chapter three.

7 Article 16 GDPR

8 Article 17 GDPR

concern about identifying whether and how such bias has taken place, which is often very hard to determine, particularly when machine learning technology is involved. Bias and discrimination are key areas which demand further research from machine learning scientists to develop solutions that can audit – or provide a full explanation for – their decisions. As we learned in Chapters one and two the industry is not yet in a position to find convincing technological solutions to provide this explanatory functionality, especially where "*black box*" AI systems are used, although there are clear industry research initiatives to enable it.

The Equality Act 2010

The other potential legal consequences that should be considered in relation to the use of artificially intelligent systems in the UK revolve principally around the Equality Act 2010.

The Equality Act is a consolidating measure in the UK which brings together the former principles set out in predecessor legislation: the Equal Pay Act 1970, the Sex Discrimination Act 1975, the Race Relations Act 1976 and the Disability Discrimination Act 1995, as well as updating the law to provide for age discrimination.

Undoubtedly the Equality Act has a part to play in determining whether or not discrimination has taken place in the workplace and in wider society – its provisions are particularly relevant to the issue of automated bias that are the subject of this chapter. There is a substantial concern however that the law as drafted however does not *explicitly* allow for a right to understand the basis for decisions made by machine learning systems.[9] The Equality Act is frustratingly unclear when it discusses burden of proof in relation to prohibited conduct, particularly when considering the nature and circumstances of algorithmic selection and decision making by artificially intelligent systems which (as we have

---

9   See for example the report of the Future of Work Commission, December 2017 (commissioned by the Labour Party)

already discussed in the context of Chapter two above) do not directly translate human actions into machine outputs. Section 136 of the Act for example provides that "*If there are facts from which the court would decide, in the absence of any other explanation, that person (A) contravened the provision concerned, the court must hold that the contravention occurred.*"[10]. Generally Section 136 dictates an absolutist and relatively unsubtle approach – it does not really address concerns about AI transparency – the use of automated machine learning tools to make opaque selection decisions which could potentially be discriminatory and where the direct human intervention in such decisions may be limited.

Until this position is clarified, we are in the awkward position of relying on the general rights we have described above under the GDPR and extrapolating the Equality Act's current drafting into our immediate context to see how it might apply. As before, our discussion is based on an analysis of the use of machine learning technologies in this context and I do not propose to provide a comprehensive summary of the Act.

What we are concerned about here is the potential for an AI system that is responsible for decision making, choices and selection to directly or indirectly discriminate against an individual's "*protected characteristics*", as these are defined through the introduction of bias in training or operational data. We have already established the potential for such machine learning systems to make decisions which due to the complexity of their processing capabilities can be incredibly difficult to rationalise on a human explicable basis and also that the learned behaviours they exhibit can "*skew*" decisions in a particular direction (the so-called *filter bubble* effect we discussed earlier).

The Equality Act itself creates a number of obligations which can lead to civil and potential criminal consequences. Criminal causation and artificial intelligence is a topic we consider specifically in Chapter six – which should be reviewed if you are interested in a more in-depth analysis of machine commissioned offences. So far as this chapter is concerned, we'll consider the prohibited acts contemplated by the Act

---

10 s136 (2)

and the provisions of Schedule 25[11], which provide some indirect pointers as to what types of machine processing are specifically excluded from its provisions.

The Equality Act makes the following "*protected characteristics*" – age[12], disability[13], gender reassignment[14], marriage and civil partnership[15], race[16], religion or belief[17], sex[18] and sexual orientation[19]. It then specifies several types of prohibited conduct in relation to those protected characteristics, which fall within Direct Discrimination[20] – being treated less favourably directly or overtly on the basis of possessing one of these protected characteristics (for example being denied a promotion on the basis of homosexuality) and Indirect Discrimination[21] – often unintended, where a provision, criterion or practice is applied equally to a group but which will ostensibly have the indirect effect of putting those who have the protected characteristic at a disadvantage.

Indirect discrimination is probably the most concerning from the perspective of machine learning given our description above, in that it is the situation which is most likely to occur when a generalised algorithmic approach is applied to a class of people. It is also worth

---

11 Information Society Service Providers

12 s5

13 s6

14 s7

15 s8

16 s9

17 s10

18 s11

19 s12

20 s13

21 s19

mentioning that there are additional prohibited acts relating to Harassment[22] and Victimisation[23].

The Act applies to those parties carrying out the prohibited conduct (generally in an employment context, this will be an employer) but in addition also applies to "*service providers*". Service Providers are defined as those " ...*concerned with the provision of a service to the public or a section of the public (for payment or not)*"[24].

It is important to note that a service provider for the purposes of the Act may not necessarily correspond with an AI provider in the narrow sense that we are discussing for the purposes of this chapter, but equally speaking *might*.

Service providers under the Equality Act provide any service. So for example when in 2015 a female paediatrician was allegedly unable to access the female changing rooms at her gym (because the automated swipe card system had incorrectly correlated the title "Dr" to exclusively male members), the Gym provider (the service provider) could have been liable for directly discriminating against her on the basis of her sex.

The provider of an AI system could conceivably be a service provider for the purposes of the Equality Act if offering a service directly to the public. In a non-public context (for example, where an employer has licensed the use of a machine learning system as a tool for use within its own business), it seems likely that the employer will also be fixed with liability for the consequences of the machine learning system in addition to any potential liability which the AI provider might also accrue. Section 109(2) of the Equality Act provides that "*Anything done by an agent for a principal, with the authority of the principal, must be treated as **also** being done by the principal*" (emphasis added).

---

22 s26

23 s27

24 s29

For the purposes of the Act, there is an important liability distinction as between service providers and employers in that whilst employers have a defence to a claim for discrimination on the basis that they take all reasonable steps to prevent it from arising[25], service providers are automatically fixed with the consequences of using technology. In practical terms this means of course that such service providers should consider very carefully the use of such technology in the provision of their service. As we have already seen, given the very complex nature of artificially intelligent systems it would be prudent in such circumstances for guarantees to be obtained from the machine learning provider that there are no instances of inbuilt bias or prejudice in their system and if and to the extent such does occur, contractual remedies, such as indemnities and other financial recompense, should be available.

Service providers may avoid liability under the Equality Act if they fall within the definition of "*Information Society Service Providers*" under Schedule 25, but in practical terms it seems clear that any utility of this provision to artificial intelligence providers is vanishingly slight.

Information Society Services are defined by the UK E-Commerce regulations[26] as "*any service normally provided for remuneration at a distance, by means of electronic equipment for the processing (including digital compression) and storage of data, at the individual request of a recipient of the service.*" Obviously the provisions of the Equality Act and the E-Commerce regulations were drafted before the advent of meaningful developments in artificial intelligence and machine learning. Some machine learning solutions will not fall within this definition, but it is conceivable that a subscription based machine learning service might. At the time Schedule 25 was intended to ensure that most online businesses within the EU were excluded from the operation of the Equality Act to the extent they were acting as a "*mere conduit*"[27] – providing access to a communications network or transmission within a commu-

---

25 s109(4)

26 Electronic Commerce (EC Directive) Regulations 2002 implementing the EU Electronic Commerce Directive 2002, repeated in Schedule 25 paragraph 7 (1) (2) (b)

nication network of information; a *"cache"*[28] – providing a temporary storage facility purely to facilitate the onwards transmission of inform- ation or a *"host"*[29] – storing information provided by a recipient of the service.

Crucially for the purposes of our analysis, Schedule 25 exemptions are removed in the case of conduits *"if the information is stored for longer than is reasonably necessary for the transmission"*[30] and in the case of caching if the service provider *"does not modify the information"*[31], both conditions of which it seems likely would be transgressed by the pro- vider of a typical AI system.

"Fake News" and other data biases

The foregoing sections of this chapter cover laws on discrimination gen- erally – assessing liability for the users of AI systems that make decisions which have *real* and significant consequences for *real* people. One should not however underestimate the potential for machine learning to continue to permeate within and influence other aspects of our lives less directly and in doing so the corresponding potential for it to spread *"data bias"* as well.

One particular example springs to mind – new digital media is a specific case in point where the assembly of "custom" news items can lead to the filter bubble effect we described above. In more extreme cases there is the potential for ill-intentioned state actors to influence media content by so called "fake news" – indeed there continues to be much publicity to this effect in relation to the US presidential election of 2016.

---

27 Paragraph 3, Schedule 25 EA 2010

28 Paragraph 4, Schedule 25 EA 2010

29 Paragraph 5, Schedule 25 EA 2010

30 Paragraph 3 (4), Schedule 25

31 Paragraph 4 (3) (a), Schedule 25

Artificially intelligent machines are taking increasing responsibility for actually writing and assembling "news" or social media items automatically and are capable of expertly manipulating photo-realistic images with no noticeable artefacts. As we saw in Chapter four, this has been taken to extreme lengths recently through the creation of machine learning neural network software that can be trained to substitute one face for another in a segment of video – so called "*deep fakes*", some of which are extremely convincing and latterly disturbing.

CHAPTER SIX
AI CRIME: COMMISSION
AND JUDGMENT

We look at two aspects of criminal liability in this chapter. The first is to examine the realistic potential for artificially intelligent systems to be liable under criminal law for the commission of an offence. The second, and I suspect rather less theoretical question, is to examine the extent to which artificial intelligence systems are influencing sentencing and bail decisions made in relation to those within the criminal justice system.

In Chapter two we looked at the legal theory of causation in a civil context – principally through the filters of tort, contract and product liability. Criminal causation is inevitably and inexorably linked to this discussion. Necessarily our debate will touch on robots in addition to artificial intelligence. As we discovered in Chapter one, modern day robots may share some characteristics with disembodied machine learning systems if they have enabled machine learning software elements – the additional factor of course is that they interact *physically* with the real world which gives them the potential to undertake *physical* acts which could lead to criminal consequences in the real world.

Pure machine learning systems in contrast are constrained by digital barriers in relation to the criminal consequences they could potentially create, although given current cybercrime levels this does not make an analysis of such systems in this context any less relevant, particularly so as those digital barriers become more permeable and connectivity between systems and smart-functionality becomes more and more ubiquitous.

Crimes at their most basic interpretation are of course acts which society has deemed – either through the application of common law or by statute – as abhorrent or contrary to the normal functioning of society, the commission of which brings about a punitive consequence. Taking aside strict liability offences, there are three basic prerequisites for criminal liability to be established in human actors – the *Actus Reus*

– or criminal act; the *Mens Rea* – or criminal intent (the so called guilty mind), and *concurrence* or *coincidence* – the coincidence of both of the former. Liability cannot be established generally unless the actor has a guilty mind and in tandem perpetrates the criminal deed.

The Actus Reas element as we know can be expressed by acts or omissions and the Mens Rea element has various levels ranging from knowledge and specific intent all the way to criminal negligence or "recklessness".

So far as machine based liability itself is concerned, there are essentially three models which have been debated by commentators and bear analysis – the first does not impute any special characteristics to the AI system.

Instrumental extension

The "*instrumental extension*" model treats AI as a tool or instrumental extension of the perpetrator, which is where the real criminal liability is focussed. This model works well, as in civil causation, where the actions of the machine are directly attributable to the actions of its user. Conventional computers, and indeed most inanimate objects, are particularly suited to this linear causality. Take for example the scenario of an entirely "dumb" factory robot, which through the direct controlled actions of its user, manages to kill a factory worker. The robot here has direct equivalence with a knife or a gun. Provided the user has the requisite *mens rea*, it seems likely that the elements of murder will be established.

The requirement of concurrence has also evolved in English jurisprudence to cover not just temporal concurrence but also motivational concurrence – provided that the guilty actor has the motivation to carry out the crime, it is not necessary for the *actus reus* to coincide in time. Many crimes are in fact the product of a sequence of connected events leading to the commission of an offence[1]. Taking our earlier example of a "dumb" robot, it seems likely therefore that even if our user had pro-grammed the robot *earlier* to behave in a particular way likely to cause the death of the factory worker (in the full knowledge that the factory worker would be present at that time) he would not escape criminal liability.

Machine Learning systems however are one step removed from this. As we have seen, they are not directly programmed but rather trained, over a period of time, in relation to a particular task. As we discussed in Chapter five, their learning can be influenced by appropriate data sets but their behaviours (or outputs) are not directed by prescriptive pro-grammed instructions. By their very nature, many such systems are inherently opaque. There are of course likely to be examples of crimin-ality where this disconnection will be problematic from an evidential point of view – especially if for example, the object of the criminal actors is to use machine learning tools to obfuscate or hide their criminal activities and more specifically (and problematically) their criminal *intent* – e.g. in a complex money laundering case (in this regard it is important to remember the distinction between burdens of proof in criminal cases and civil ones – whereas a civil case need be proved only on a *balance of probabilities*, the evidential burden in criminal cases is much higher – *beyond reasonable doubt*).

In other cases however, this disconnect is likely to be relatively mean-ingless given the context and circumstances – take the recent 2015 case (publicised somewhat melodramatically in the media as "*Robot gets arrested*") of a Swiss art collective that used an intelligent "bot" armed with $100 worth of bitcoin to purchase Ecstasy tablets, a Hungarian Passport and various spying devices as part of an art installation on the power of the so called "Dark Web". The system (the so called "*Random Dark Net Shopper*") purchased the items and had them delivered to the art gallery – a relatively easy way to track down the perpetrators.[2]

---

1   See for example *R v. Le Brun [1991] CA*; *R v. Jakeman (1982) CA*; *Fagan v. Metropolitan Police Commissioner [1968] QBD*

Natural and probable consequences

The next model which has been proposed in the context of machine liability is what is termed the *"natural probable consequences"* model. I should say at the outset that this is a highly problematic doctrine in its own right and has been largely discredited in many US states, as well as comparable jurisdictions, such as the UK which expressly prohibited its application by s8 of the Criminal Justice Act 1967[3].

In this model, the AI system takes action which is a *"natural and probable"* consequence of its training. So going back to our earlier example of the robot killing a factory worker, (assuming our machine now has artificial intelligence capabilities), in this model, the creator of the artificially intelligent system does not need to have a specific intent (or *mens rea*) to kill the factory worker, but rather a state of criminal negligence – that is to say reckless disregard as to whether the training of the machine learning system could lead to the death of the factory worker – if a reasonable person in the place of the creator could have forseen the offence as a *natural probable consequence* of the way in which the process was conducted. The doctrine evolved as a way to embrace accomplice liability (i.e. where there been offence committed by an accomplice which is not part of a conspiracy, but which would otherwise be a "natural probable consequence" of a criminal scheme) and essentially side steps the subjective requirement for juries to assess whether or not the guilty party possessed the necessary mens rea. Ironically, given the difficulties we have discussed above in relation to the opaque way in which machine learning systems operate, this doctrine (although effectively discredited) might in fact provide a more convenient route for the judicial system to establish appropriate criminal liability in cases where artificially intelligent systems have been used in the commission of an offence.

---

2   See Guardian dated 22 April 2015 *"Swiss Police release robot that bought ecstasy online"*

3   s8 of the 1967 Act reversed the position reached in *DPP v. Smith (1961) AC 290* which originally proposed a "natural and probable consequences" test as a means to attempt to objectively translate criminal recklessness into intent

Direct machine liability

Finally, there is the theoretical possibility of a criminal liability model which assumes some level of responsibility *per se* on the part of the machine for its actions. I refer to theoretical because, as we have learned, liability and accountability both require some element of understanding and self-awareness on the part of the artificially intelligent system for the consequences of its actions.

To a certain degree this plays back to our debate on individuation in the context of civil causation in Chapter two. Despite the views of many populist commentators, we are not currently at a technological state of the art where this is relevant.

How then should the criminal justice system respond to increasingly complex crimes in which increasingly complex machines play significant parts? The response must logically be dictated in a similar manner to the conclusions I reach in Chapter two – if the natural and probable consequence doctrine cannot be reinvigorated in criminal situations where machine intelligence is deployed, potentially making the issue of determining whether the alleged defendants to a crime have the requisite *mens rea,* then the response of the legislators has to be to consider an increase in the scope of strict liability offences.

Strict liability

Generally strict liability offences are those under which intention does not have to be proven in relation to an aspect of the *actus reus*, although some element of intent may be required in relation to the other aspects of the offence in question – such as recklessness. Strict liability offences are as a rule created by Statute – however typically, Parliament does not make it expressly clear in most instances whether an offence should be one of strict liability. Indeed this may be an unintended consequence of some Acts which are poorly drafted or vague in their approach.

The courts apply several principles to override the general presumption of *mens rea* to establish strict liability[4]. For the purposes of our current analysis, it makes sense to focus on these principles which are likely to come into sharp focus in circumstances where use of intelligent machines cause injury or loss, and that is where a statutory offence is dealing with an issue of social concern.

The leading case of *Gammon (Hong Kong) v. AG*[5] provides that where a statute is legislating on an issue of social concern, and the creation of strict liability will promote the purpose of the statute by encouraging individuals to take extra measures against committing the offence, the general presumption in favour of mens rea can be rebutted.

Typically the courts will not make this leap where the offence is a "real" crime with moral consequences as opposed to an offence which is regulatory in nature[6] (usually one where no moral issues are involved) or one which carries serious penalties – generally they are more willing to do so in cases where the penalties for breach are relatively small – but this is not a rule which is applied prescriptively.

The Gammon case concerned a failure on the part of the defendants to follow building plans accurately (due to the imposition of changes) which caused a major building collapse in Hong Kong. Under the relevant building and construction regulations there was a maximum penalty for breach of up to three years in prison or a fine of $250,000. The Privy Council upheld the view that the offence was one of strict liability and it did not matter whether the defendants were aware that their changes may have led to the collapse.

As the use of artificially intelligent systems becomes more pervasive in society, so inevitably the tendency of the clever and ill-intentioned to avoid criminal sanctions will increase commensurately and of course in

---

4 In *B (a minor) v. DPP (2000)*

5 [1985] AC 1

6 See *Sweet v. Parsley [1970] AC 132*

many clever, convoluted and devious ways that cannot be predicted. The extension of strict liability provides society with an organic and flexible response to these changing circumstances which does not necessitate a wholesale change to the way in which we judge criminal accountability.

The criminal justice system – bail and sentencing decisions

The second part of this chapter takes a look at the increasing use of machine learning systems in the criminal justice system – specifically in relation to the sentencing of crimes. The increased uptake of such systems raises the spectres of bias, discrimination and accountability (and the increased potential for claims which are based on the misuse of such systems) which we have discussed in previous chapters but which it is important to discuss in the context of crime.

In the criminal justice system, artificial intelligence is now being used in the United States to make sentencing, bail and parole decisions for prisoners (such technology is at present being trialled in the UK). The recent US criminal case of *State v. Loomis*[7], provides a somewhat worrying example of the rise of such technology (and the court's attitude to its use). Eric Loomis was charged in early 2015 with five criminal counts in a drive by shooting in Wisconsin. In the event, the defendant pleaded guilty to two lesser of the five charges. In preparation for his sentencing hearing, the Wisconsin Department of Corrections produced a pre-sentencing investigation report (a so called "PSI"), that included an AI assessment of his potential to commit further crime.

The system used in Loomis' assessment was COMPAS, developed by Equivant. COMPAS is a decision tree based classification solution and uses interviews with offenders as well as information from their criminal records history to determine the risk of recidivism. As such it is employed primarily in the US criminal justice system to assess eligibility for parole, bail and also to determine sentencing levels.

---

7   881 N.W. 2d 749 (Wis. 2016)

Ironically, given the nature of the algorithmic solution, which is more white box than black box (see our discussion at Chapter one), both Loomis and the Court were prevented from obtaining details as to how the system had classified him for sentencing on the basis that the methodology the system used was proprietary in nature – specifically a trade secret.

The Wisconsin Supreme Court found that the defendant's due process had not been violated by use of an algorithmic sentencing system, even though it was not made clear to the defendant or the court *how* it had reached the conclusions it had in his particular case. Instead, the court ruled that any future use of such automated assessments needed to be subject to notification of certain "health warnings". These health warnings should be directed to the court reviewing the system's decisions in any particular situation in order to prevent blind acceptance of its findings and to introduce a degree of judicial scepticism. Whilst this approach clearly acknowledges the risk of relying on algorithmic risk assessment, it provided cold comfort for the defendant in the Loomis case. It is particularly interesting to note that this case is unlikely to have been decided in an equivalent manner in the EU – even if perhaps the outcome of the case might have been the same.

Article 22 of the GDPR on Automated Decision making and profiling prevents (as we have seen previously in Chapter three) cursory human involvement in such decision making and would require active and participative involvement in the part of the judges involved when making a sentencing decision.

CHAPTER SEVEN
MARKET DISTORTING EFFECTS:
AI AND COMPETITION LAW

Competition and trade sit at the heart of western democratic societies. The fundamental principles enshrined in the European Union's 1958 Treaty of Rome – now the "*TFEU*" or "*Treaty on the functioning of the EU*" have as their bases the general aspiration that within the European Union, trade should be unfettered and that goods and services be allowed to develop market equilibrium free of behaviours such as organised *cartels* (companies coming together in a concerted fashion to maintain or fix prices or share markets or customers or otherwise distort market forces) or the *abuse of a dominant market position* (using a monopoly position to exploit customers or to entrench that monopoly).

Again, I do not propose within this chapter to provide a detailed guide to competition law (there are other more detailed texts which achieve this aim), but rather to contextualise our debate on machine learning within the framework of competition law rules and provide you the reader with an appreciation of the issues which might apply when using AI tools in this setting. Competition law is a public interest driven exception to the principle of freedom of contract. Effective competition typically drives lower prices, better quality and choice and more innovation, so it is in the public – (ie. the consumer's) interest that companies do not co-operate or collude in ways which impede the free play of those market forces of competition.

Powerful machine learning tools can be deployed to increase the individual economic efficiency of undertakings: reducing your cost base is a pro-competitive move which (absent dominance), competition law will not interfere with. But if such tools are used in a co-ordinated way, or if the agreement between the business and the AI supplier contains restrictions on competition (such as, for example, exclusivity provisions or "*most favoured customer*" clauses, then there may be regulatory tension in relation to the permissible use of such tools in an economic context.

Article 101(1) TFEU provides that "*The following shall be prohibited as incompatible with the internal market: all agreements between under-takings, decisions by associations of undertakings and concerted practices which may affect trade between Member States and which have as their object or effect the prevention, restriction or distortion of competition…and in particular those which: (a) directly or indirectly fix purchase or selling prices…; (b) limit or control production, markets, technical development, or investment; (c) share markets or sources of supply; [and/or] (d) apply dis-similar conditions to equivalent transactions with other trading parties, thereby placing them at a competitive disadvantage; (e)…*".* Article 101(3) provides for the derogation to this overarching principle (where the agreement, decision or concerted practice of undertakings may be allowed) if it "*contributes to improving the production or distribution of goods or to promoting technical or economic progress, while allowing con-sumers a fair share of the resulting benefit*" and does not either impose unnecessary restrictions (ie. those indispensable to the objectives expressed in Article 101(3))[1] or provide such undertakings with the pos-sibility of "*eliminating competition*" for a substantial part of the products in question[2]. Article 102 TFEU then goes on to explain the European Union position on abuses of a dominant market position: "*Any abuse by one or more undertakings of a dominant position within the internal market … shall be prohibited as incompatible with the internal market in so far as it may affect trade between Member States. Such abuse may, in particular, consist in: (a) directly or indirectly imposing unfair purchase or selling prices or other unfair trading conditions; (b) limiting production, markets or technical development to the prejudice of consumers; [and/or] (c) applying dissimilar conditions to equivalent transactions with other trading parties, thereby placing them at a competitive disadvantage; (d) ….*".* There are derogations from these overarching principles (such as for example in relation to agricultural trade between the EU Member States – protecting the Common Agricultural Policy; in relation to the Defence industry; and finally intellectual property licensing), but I do not propose to dwell on these here. Additionally, the United States has

---

1 See Article 101(3)(a) TFEU

2 See Article 101(3)(B) TFEU

similar, but not precisely equivalent provisions in its anti-trust legislation, predominantly enshrined in the Sherman Act[3].

The essential question to understand for the purposes of this text is to understand how the use of machine learning tools can undermine these central principles and if so, in what manner. The essence of our debate in this context has similarities with, and draws from, our previous discussions in relation to bias and discrimination (Chapter five) and big data (Chapter three). Put simply, machine learning systems have the ability to analyse and correlate hugely complex pools of data and review dimensionalities in such data which are far beyond what could be achieved by humans in any realistic timeline.

As we move completely into digital data processing and away from an essentially analog documentary existence, vast amounts of data have become available to information processing systems. It is not just the ability to spot patterns at a superhuman level which is interesting from a competition law perspective, but also the ability of such systems to make autonomous decisions and react on the basis of such data almost instantaneously.

Pro-competitive vs. anti-competitive effects

In many situations the availability of online tools, such as price aggregation services and online commerce platforms drive healthy competition by forcing the market to respond in a number of ways: by for example, increasing pricing transparency and creating new routes to market for smaller businesses, reducing barriers to entry in a market place. To take a particular example if (ignoring for the moment the numerous regulatory hurdles involved) you have a mobile phone and a car, you can now compete with a taxi driver through driving apps such as Uber.

Product and service aggregation sites can act to facilitate competition by providing consumers with more easily accessible choice (indeed in some

---

3   See sections 1 and 2 of the Sherman Act 1890

markets we now have aggregators that sit over multiple other aggregators to further enhance choice and price, such as SkyScanner, which essentially "sweeps" price aggregation data for airline tickets and flights from other aggregators). Finally artificial intelligence is fuelling an increasingly dynamic environment where pricing for goods and services can be adjusted in accordance with a number of complex external supply and demand factors – both actual and now predicted, on a near instantaneous basis to ensure that the most competitive pricing is offered in a way that would be inconceivable in a predominantly physical ("*bricks and mortar*") environment.

This essentially pro-competitive and beneficial view of digital competitive trends is however qualified by the reality of many competitive market places which are dominated by a single monopolistic, or a few large oligopolistic, players. Businesses such as Google have seen significant fines for behaviour which the European Commission judges to be anti-competitive and damaging to its customers and/or the structure of competition.

Companies are increasingly realising that big data is the fuel that drives their businesses and the key which will enable them to unlock more business and outperform their competitors. In many areas of modern business therefore it is as much about a race to obtain and secure large amounts of data in relation to the consumers of your products and services as it is about identifying pricing trends in those items.

Artificially intelligent systems put data acquisition and data manipulation on another, higher, much more sophisticated plane – not only can they analyse data as I have already described, but now they can also apply analytics to synthesise or predict data (as we saw in the context of Chapter three above) which will determine pricing, availability, demand trends and other likely contextual information about the goods and services in question. Indeed, algorithmic systems are now being used to "*micro target*" consumers so that it is possible that you will be offered different pricing (when compared to another consumer) for the same service or product based on your perceived demand for it or some other characteristic, such as where you live, or be offered complementary products to those you have actually purchased.

Consider as well that much of this sophistication is offered within *"walled-garden"* ecosystems that have been developed by companies such as Amazon and eBay which have become so powerful that they cannot be ignored by other retailers (who in consequence, have to join them) and rather than enhanced competition, what might be happening is a recipe for consumers to have their choices limited either because they become bound to a single dominant marketplace or in the alternative are limited to using a few dominant players in an oligopoly.

In each case listed above there is in fact limited or no effective price competition – either because in the former, the *walled garden* can ultimately determine its own price equilibrium, which could potentially signal price monopolisation or in the latter where our oligopolistic players reach price stabilisation (or *harmonised* prices), not through any overt collusive activity, but simply because the algorithmic systems used by them have reached the same conclusion – in competition terms, through a process of *unconscious parallelism*.

These are of course polarised examples of the potential market effects of AI on economic activity – the world is a messy place and in reality the effect of artificial intelligence systems on trade and competition will need to be assessed on the facts of the individual case. We have not yet reached a unity in the deployment of artificial intelligence systems or indeed in terms of utilised data sets – as we have seen there are a variety of technological solutions being continuously developed and enhanced, and the reality is that different businesses gain different advantages from the use of these new tools. Such price and cost asymmetries will aid in the maintenance of a healthily competitive market. On the other hand, we cannot ignore the fact that in many markets the cost of entry is increasingly being driven by big data acquisition which, of itself, could prove a much higher barrier.

One of the biggest issues for anti-trust regulators in this context will of course be to spot and identify potentially insidious *automated* anti-competitive behaviours as we increasingly move into a digitalised environment.

Competition and anti-trust law has a long history both in Europe and the United States – certainly reaching back before the advent of digital computers. Some argue that Competition authorities are increasingly becoming less capable of taking on anti-competitive behaviours which will ultimately harm consumers because economic activity is transitioning away from the human physical medium towards a digital environment which takes place within and between autonomous machines.

One of the best ways to illustrate this transition and to show how artificial intelligence is potentially at both a competition enabler and blocker is to look at an industry specific contextual example. As we saw in Chapter three, in the context of our discussion on big data, the insurance industry has been one of the trailblazers for use of machine learning technology. Artificial intelligence is rapidly transforming the way in which insurance is priced, quoted for and underwritten. Increasing sophistication is allowing new insurance intermediary start-ups to model synthetic claims data to enable much more accurate pricing of risk. As these intermediaries gather more and more actual claims data (and more insurers participate in these intermediary platforms), their machine learning solutions become ever more accurate. The competitive impact of such tools depends upon who is deploying them: access to smaller underwriters may enable them to compete more effectively in the market – effectively levelling the playing field, whilst price competition between the larger players may reduce if multiple parties use the same algorithmic pricing output.

Regulatory Responses

What to date then has the response been of the Competition authorities to the use of artificial intelligence and machine learning?

To date there has been a paucity of officially reported cases considering the effect of machine learning in a competition scenario. In the UK the competition authorities have considered a case where price matching algorithms were used to implement a cartel between Amazon market-place competitors, but no cases have yet been considered where the issue of parallel, algorithm driven pricing has been considered, or where machine learning solutions have "independently" arrived at a cartelised price. No doubt in anticipation of a potential flood of such cases, a consultation document has been recently published by the OECD containing representations from the competition and anti-trust authorities EU, Italy, Russia, the UK and the United States (amongst others) on the potential threats posed by algorithmic collusion[4].

This gives a useful view as to how major regulators across the globe will respond to this particular challenge – although unfortunately many of the responses are less than insightful. The European Union's response is to confirm that if an activity is illegal offline it will also be illegal online and such systems remain under the "*direction and control*" of the firm using it. It observes that algorithmic systems may be used differently in vertical and horizontal contexts (*vertical* context being an arrangement at different levels within a supply chain, such as supplier and distributor and *horizontal* context referring to an arrangement at the same level, such as those between competitors). Vertical usage could provide suppliers with tools to monitor fixed, minimum or recommended prices so as to exercise pressure on or provide incentives to retailers (potentially a step towards illegal resale price maintenance) whilst horizontal usage could be deployed to monitor competitor pricing (not of itself illegal) and to ultimately potentially facilitate collusion[5].

The OECD report does not address the difficulties involved in identifying such behaviours in the first place or whether indeed an artificially intelligent system managing pricing algorithms is "*under the control*" of the firm using it. In fact it seems probable that regulators will determine

---

4   Algorithms and Collusion – Summaries of Contributions, OECD 21-23 June 2017, DAF/COMP/WD(2017) 2

5   Page 4, ibid.

that such systems are under the control of the firms using them as this conclusion provides them with a target to apply fines.

Both the UK[6] and the Italian[7] regulators pick up policing concerns (reflected as themes previously referred to in this chapter) which identify concerns in relation to self-learning algorithmic systems that are less dependent upon (and arguably less subject to) direct human control, and the US Federal Trade Commission[8] makes the point (again reflected earlier in this chapter) that price stabilisation may occur even where there is no direct collusion between firms where for example they purchase the same algorithmic solution, which is reliant on the same data sets.

Undoubtedly regulators are live to the issues involved in the use of potentially autonomous agents in a competition context – the big question for the immediate and near-term future is the extent to which they will be able to identify anti-competitive behaviours and enforce them within existing competition law frameworks.

---

6 Page 9, ibid.

7 Page 5, ibid.

8 Page 10, ibid.

CHAPTER EIGHT
SECTOR SPECIFIC
CONSIDERATIONS

In this chapter we take a closer look at some additional legal considerations for Artificial Intelligence and machine learning in relation to particular sector-based applications.

Specifically we consider how machine learning is influencing the delivery of medicine and healthcare, as well as the disruption this technology is bringing to the retail, financial services, transportation and energy and infrastructure industries.

Lifesciences, Medicine and Healthcare

Artificial intelligence is bringing to life some particularly exciting applications in relation to the practice of medicine.

Broadly speaking, the AI applications in this sector can be divided into the following categories (and I have deliberately excluded drug discovery or pharmacological based innovation from this analysis): diagnostic classification or prediction through systematic review of patient related evidence such as medical imaging or symptomatic patient data, where the power of deep learning is harnessed to better identify the presence of or predict the incidence of disease; and IoT or *"internet of things"* chronic disease management systems, where AI powered applications monitor patient health and manage chronic conditions through automated drug delivery and regular information updates to healthcare professionals. It is in the first category that some of the most startling achievements have been made. "Deep Patient" for example, a program developed by researchers at Mount Sinai Hospital in New York, was provided with the records of 700,000 individuals as a training data set with a view to predicting disease in patients at the hospital. When presented with new records for examination, it proved to be very accurate – sometimes even accurately predicting disease incidence for highly unpredictable conditions, such as schizophrenia that human medical professionals had difficulty in doing[1].

For now, the "*holy grail*" of direct surgical intervention (robotic surgery) where trained robots autonomously perform actual medical operations remains science fiction rather than fact, despite some interesting research which shows promise in the technology. The Da Vinci surgical robot, for example, which has been on the market for the last 15 years – actually depends upon remote actuation by human surgeon and "tunes out" autonomous movement on the basis that all procedures should be human directed.

Personal Data regulation – and in particular the GDPR (General Data Protection Regulation) features large in terms of the use of such applications, particularly when one considers that much of their utility is based on the treatment of individuals. Chapter three of this book (on Big Data and Artificial Intelligence) considers such regulation at length, however for the purposes of this chapter it is worth noting that a similar experiment to the one carried out at Mount Sinai hospital was attempted in the UK by the Royal Free NHS Foundation Trust – a collective of three major London hospitals. The Royal Free trust handed over 1.6 million patient records to Google's DeepMind project with a view to testing a system for detection and diagnosis of acute kidney injury. The UK's ICO ruled, when looking at the essential seven data protection principles, that this had been done in contravention of the Data Protection Act as, amongst other grounds, there was a lack of transparency in how the data used would be processed and insufficient measures had been taken to inform patients that their data would be used in clinical safety testing. In consequence, it was not reasonable to expect them to understand that their data would be used in this way. The ICO also found that the use of 1.6 million patient records was excessive and disproportionate. The Royal Free trust was ultimately

---

1 Deep Patient: An Unsupervised Representation to Predict the Future of Patients from the Electronic Health Records, Miotto, Li, Kidd & Dudley, Scientific Reports 2016

asked to sign an undertaking in relation to its future use of patient data and to commission a third-party audit of the DeepMind trial.

In addition to data protection regulation, it is probably medical device regulation which impacts most upon the use of AI applications in this sector. EU regulation in this space is driven by a suite of Medical Device Directives[2], which are due to be supplanted in 2020 and 2022 respectively by a new Regulation on Medical Devices[3] and another on In Vitro Diagnostic Medical Devices[4]. The Medical Device Directives (and the subsequent Regulations which are due to supplant them), put in place a CE declaration of conformity scheme in respect of such devices which is in effect a mandatory quality assurance scheme to minimise risk and maximise safety in relation to their production, distribution, storage and use. The new Regulations maintain and strengthen this regime through the introduction of a harmonised EU approach, increase transparency by the introduction of an EU wide database of such devices to ensure transparency as well as bringing in new post and pre-market reporting and surveillance measures.

A "medical device" is defined by the current legislation as "*any instrument, apparatus, appliance, software, material or other article, whether used alone or in combination, including the software intended by its manufacturer to be used specifically for diagnostic and/or therapeutic purposes and necessary for its proper application, intended by the manufacturer to be used for human beings for the purpose of: — diagnosis, prevention, monitoring, treatment or alleviation of disease, diagnosis, monitoring, treatment, alleviation of or compensation for an injury or handicap, investigation, replacement or modification of the anatomy or of a physiological process, control of conception, and which does not achieve its principal intended action in or on the human body by pharmacological,*

---

2 Directive 90/385/EEC on Active Implantable Medical Devices, Directive 93/42/EEC on Medical Devices and Directive 98/79/EC on In Vitro Diagnostic Medical Devices

3 Regulation EU 2017/745

4 Regulation EU 2017/746

immunological or metabolic means, but which may be assisted in its function by such means"[5]. What is interesting from our viewpoint is that the ECJ has recently issued guidance in the *Snitem/Philips France* case[6] to the effect that standalone software not embodied in an apparatus should be treated as a medical device for the purposes of the legislation if "*the intended purpose, defined by the manufacturer, is specifically medical*"[7] – it is not enough if the software is general purpose but used in a medical setting (such as for example a word processing package used in a hospital). Quite whether this provides sufficient clarity for use of Artificially intelligent software-based systems when used in a medical context remains to be seen – particularly given the potentially general purpose nature of some systems. Paradoxically we could end up in a situation where the applicability of the legislation depends upon the context – so that a neural network trained on diagnostic patient data used in a hospital for the purpose of identifying disease is caught, whereas an ostensibly identical system trained on data which is designed to optimise the efficiency and regulate the environmental controls of the hospital building is not.

Retail and Consumer

As we saw in Chapter seven (Market Distorting Effects – AI and Competition Law), much machine learning activity in the retail sector is driven by the price optimisation strategies which are being adopted by the major online retail platforms. Aside from these considerations, the sector is leading the way in machine learning powered CRM (or customer relationship management) – which could include the provision of chat bots or interactive intelligent customer platforms to assist in a pre or post sales environment or automated product recommendations. Artificial Intelligence is also optimising manufacturing, logistics and delivery and payment processes.

---

5   Article 1 2)(a) of Directive 93/42/EEC

6   C-329/16

7   C-329/16 at paragraph 24

As with Medicine and Healthcare, much innovation in retail is also being driven by the increased sophistication with which machine learning applications can process personal data, so the topics debated in Chapter three (Big Data and Artificial Intelligence) are equally relevant here.

Aside from this, consumer and retail related regulation in the UK is focussed on consumer protection law (principally the Consumer Protection Act 1987) and consumer rights (the Consumer Rights Act 2015), both of which were discussed in detail in Chapter two (Causation and Artificial Intelligence) in the context of contractually based causation. The one area which is worth raising here are the new provisions in the Consumer Rights Act which may apply in a context where artificial intelligence solutions are being used in a retail context. Chapter 3 of that Act puts in place a range of provisions which relate to the supply of digital content and digital services[8]. Clearly these provisions are not intended merely to apply to machine learning solutions but in relation to anything which is supplied in a digital context.

Chapter 3 applies to *"a contract for a trader to supply digital content to a consumer, if it is supplied or to be supplied for a price paid by the consumer. (2) This Chapter also applies to a contract for a trader to supply digital content to a consumer, if (a) it is supplied free with goods or services or other digital content for which the consumer pays a price, and (b) it is not generally available to consumers unless they have paid a price for it or for goods or services or other digital content"*[9].

A range of familiar statutory warranties and remedies are then provided, which align broadly to the warranties and remedies originating in the Sale of Goods Act 1893 and its successor statute, the Sale of Goods Act 1979, including warranties as to conformity with description, satisfactory quality and fitness for purpose (which we will return to in a moment), and remedies that provide for a right to a repair or a

---

8   Sections 33-47 of the Consumer Rights Act, 2015

9   Sections 33(1), 33(2) (a) & (b)

replacement[10], price reduction[11] or a refund[12]. Where dealing with consumers, these provisions cannot be contracted out of.[13]

So the scope of application would apply in relation to digital content paid for directly by a consumer – typically in the form of a digital download of software, or something which is "*bundled*" with either other digital content, services or a device. Clearly therefore, and to take a specific example by way of our immediate context, the provision of an Amazon Echo device with Amazon's voice service, Alexa would be caught.

Quite how useful these provisions actually are in the context of e.g. a digital voice assistant, remains to be seen. The law inevitably pre-dates the widespread availability of these AI powered services and pre-supposes an essentially static, predictable or linear performance in relation to the relevant digital content – so that for example a downloaded digital video should *play* without interruption or a piece of games software should *install and activate* on the hardware which it is downloaded to in accordance with its specification. An NLP (natural language processing) enabled AI voice assistant will almost certainly be subject to a more complex assessment as to whether it is of "*satisfactory quality*"[14], "*fit for purpose*"[15] or "*in conformity with description*"[16]. Evidently one which does not function at all when the device within which it is installed is enabled fails these benchmarks. But what of one that lies, is inaccurate in its answers or issues profanities? These will be matters which will inevitably become the subject of future litigation.

------

10 Section 43, Consumer Rights Act 2015

11 Section 44, Consumer Rights Act 2015

12 Section 45, Consumer Rights Act 2015

13 Section 47, Consumer Rights Act 2015

14 Section 34, Consumer Rights Act 2015

15 Section 35, Consumer Rights Act 2015

16 Section 36, Consumer Rights Act 2015

It is apparent that the role of supplier statements, descriptions and disclaimers will become ever more critical in determining what is reasonable to expect when using such devices – Section 34(2) in the context of satisfactory quality provides that "*the quality of digital content is satisfactory if it meets the standard that a reasonable person would consider satisfactory, taking account of—*

(a) any description of the digital content, (b)the price mentioned in section 33(1) or (2)(b) (if relevant), and (c)all the other relevant circumstances (see subsection (5))." – Subsection (5) of the same section providing that "*the relevant circumstances mentioned in subsection (2)(c) include any public statement about the specific characteristics of the digital content made by the trader, the producer or any representative of the trader or the producer."*

Financial Services

The next sector which is worthy of some consideration is that of financial services. As we have seen in the context of some of the other discussions in this book, artificial intelligence is permeating and disrupting virtually every aspect of the financial services industry (see for example various discussions on the insurance industry in Chapters two, three and seven, above). Given the length of time that some level of automation has been available in the financial services industry, it is interesting to benchmark legislative responses in this sector against those sectors which are comparatively less mature (or at least, where machine learning solutions are considered more novel).

For the purposes of this particular section I intend however to focus briefly on two distinct aspects that are worthy of mention – one being algorithmic trading or "*robotrading*" and the other "*roboadvice*". As these names imply, these are either investment or advice-based services which are carried on fully autonomously or with some level of human intervention. It is important to note that not all of these services deploy sophisticated artificial intelligence or machine learning as part of their solution, but there is an increased tendency in the industry to do so.

Algorithmic trading exists because when used correctly, it provides significant advantages over traditional trading methods – specifically in relation to trading and execution speed and latency. These factors often make the difference between loss and profit in relation to financial trading, although there are concerns that without appropriate levels of oversight and supervision we could be led into other market falls such as the 2010 *"flash crash"* (generally accepted to have been caused by algorithmic traders), which caused a brief 36 minute crash in the Dow Jones and Nasdaq indices, momentarily causing them to lose around a trillion US dollars. The Markets in Financial Instruments Directive (or "MiFID" as it is more commonly referred to in the industry), defines algorithmic trading as *"Trading in financial instruments which meets the following conditions: (a) where a computer algorithm automatically determines individual parameters of orders such as whether to initiate the order, the timing, price or quantity of the order or how to manage the order after its submission (b) there is limited or no human intervention does not include any system that is only used for the purpose of routing orders to one or more trading venues or the processing of orders involving no determination of any trading parameters or for the confirmation of orders or the post-trade processing of executed transactions."*[17]. The legislative provisions of MiFID are sensibly pragmatic – reflecting the relative maturity of the use of such automated solutions in trading as opposed to some of the other legislative measures that we have discussed in other contexts. The MiFID requirements on algorithmic trading are embodied in UK law through the FCA's Market Conduct Sourcebook or "MAR" and the EU Commission Delegated Regulation 2017/589 which is referred to in the industry as "RTS 6". I do not propose to go into the details here but they are intended to introduce a governance and reporting framework for firms using such solutions and are designed to ensure safety (such as business continuity and *"kill switches"* where appropriate) as well as consistent systems and controls in order to prevent market abuse or disorderly markets.

Roboadvice or automated investment advice is the other area which has seen significant growth in recent years as the utility and flexibility of

---

17 Article 4(1) 39 of MiFID (2014/65/EU)

artificially intelligent powered solutions has increased. This is due to the fact that there is an increasing trend for consumers to take control of their own finances and to dispense with traditional intermediaries, such as financial advisors. In many cases, such consumers will be using online tools to determine whether or not they should invest in a particular product, and this puts the whole concept of automated advice and/or recommendations into the spotlight.

Typically the UK and European regulators makes no distinction for regulatory purposes between *investment advice* provided on a traditional basis, or via an automated solution. What has therefore been important for firms offering such *roboadvice* is determining in fact whether what they are offering is regulated investment advice and are caught by the regulatory regime, or *guidance,* which is essentially unregulated. This is often referred to as the "*advice boundary*".

Unfortunately there are differences in the way in which the "advice boundary" is determined when the relevant legislation is taken into account when one considers the two pieces of legislation that must be followed. The first is Article 53 of the existing Financial Services and Markets Act 2000 (Regulated Activities) Order 2001 (the "Regulated Activities Order" or "RAO"), and the second is MiFID. MiFID focusses on the provision of personal advice recommendations to an individual customer. The three main elements are that (i) there is a recommendation that is made to a person in their capacity as an investor or potential investor; (ii) it is based on the investor's personal circumstances and is presented as suitable when taking these personal circumstances into account; and (iii) the recommendation must relate to a type of investment which is a MiFID financial instrument[18].

The definition of advice under the RAO in contrast however is wider. This is because there is no requirement under that legislation for advice to be of a personal nature. Instead, the RAO prescribes that the fol-

---

18 See Section C, Annex I of MiFID (2014/65/EU) – generally transferrable securities, money market instruments, units in collective investment undertakings, options, futures, swaps, forward rate agreements and other derivative contracts.

lowing types of advice are regulated: such advice must (i) relate to a relevant investment[19]; (ii) be given to a person in their capacity as an investor or potential investor and (iii) relate to the buying, selling, subscribing for or underwriting that investment[20].

In 2015, the UK government launched a wide-ranging review of the market in financial advice, the so called Financial Advice Market Review or FAMR. This was in general prompted by a concern that consumers with more limited amounts to invest were suffering from a so-called investment advice gap which was limiting the quality and nature of financial advice being provided – of which roboadvice, as we have seen, plays an increasingly critical part.

FAMR identified the need to clarify the advice/guidance boundary we have described above and subsequently recommended that the definition within the RAO be aligned to the MiFID definition by new secondary legislation to enable firms to more accurately determine which side of the advice boundary their services are more likely to fall. Clearly, therefore, the provision of machine learning based guided investment tools is at an early stage – but at least in the financial services industry, as we noted at the outset of this section, there is a widespread recognition of the impact of such technologies and appropriate legislative responses are being formulated in response.

Transportation

In Chapter two, on Causation, we briefly covered on the UK government's legislative response to automation and transportation as embodied in the Autonomous and Electric Vehicles Bill which attempts to clarify potential gaps in insurance cover liability when a vehicle is

---

19 See Article 3(1) of the Financial Services and Markets Act 2000 (Regulated Activities) Order 2001, and Part 4 of the FCA's Conduct of Business Sourcebook (COBS4)

20 Article 53 of the Financial Services and Markets Act 2000 (Regulated Activities) Order 2001

being piloted autonomously as opposed to a human driver[21]. Whilst this is a pragmatic response to an immediate problem caused by the use of such vehicles, it does not, as we explained at length in Chapter two, do much more than push causation issues directly into the laps of insurers who will still face considerable difficulties in pursuing claims against other third parties, including the manufacturers of such vehicles. Chapter three, on Big Data, touched on the EU's *Strategy on Co-operative Intelligent Transport Systems (CIT-S)* which set out a policy vision in relation to smart vehicle communications infrastructure from a personal data management perspective.

Aside from these two measures, the Law Commission of England and Wales in a joint project with the Law Commission for Scotland, have, at time of writing, been tasked by the Centre for Connected and Autonomous Vehicles (which is part of the Departments for Transport and Business, Energy and Industrial Strategy) to undertake a wide ranging review of the laws relating to the regulation and review of autonomous vehicles[22], in recognition of the inadequacies in the law discussed in the earlier chapters of this book.

The review will address concerns related to safety assurance mechanisms (such as type approvals and MoTs), accountability in terms of crime and accidents, and assessing how to decide whether such vehicles are safe for road use. Data protection and privacy issues, theft and cyber security and land use policy are expressly stated to be outside of the review's scope, as are drones and vehicles which are designed solely for use on pavements rather than roads. The review will be for a three year period commencing in March 2018, and it is expected that a scoping paper for consultations will be published before the end of 2018.

---

21 Section 2 of the Autonomous and Electric Vehicles Bill

22 See https://www.lawcom.gov.uk/project/automated-vehicles/

Energy and Utilities

The energy sector has all the characteristics which would lend itself to effective implementation of machine learning technologies – the sector relies on a very large generation and distribution infrastructure – and also deals with significant amounts of personal data from consumers of those utilities. Automated trading in energy-based commodities is of course caught by the financial services considerations we discussed earlier in this chapter, and the use of artificially intelligent systems to price or recommend energy supplier "switches" for retail consumers may also touch the Competition considerations we looked at in the context of Chapter seven, although it is worth bearing in mind that wholesale gas and electricity generation and distribution markets in the UK are monopolistic and that the regulator, Ofgem, has interposed itself into these by the imposition of price controls on transmission and distribution.

To date, there have been limited forays – smart home automation, both in terms of monitoring usage by way of *IoT* or *Internet of Things* enabled intelligent thermostatic devices and metering – so called "smart meters" are beginning to penetrate households and raise the same privacy and data protection implications for personal data management that we discussed in Chapter three.

"Smart grid" management of power distribution has the potential to revolutionise energy management from an environmental, cost and demand perspective, by for example increasing output when needed (or anticipating such spikes in demand) or shuttling capacity intelligently to where it is needed the most. Such smart grid technologies also have the benefit of potentially offering more sophisticated "real time" maintenance management (for example by reporting and predicting network points of failure) as well as providing enhanced monitoring to enable protection against what are perceived as an increased level of cyber security threats that threaten the integrity of utility networks. As of the date of writing, there are no specific legislative measures in contemplation within the UK to cover the use of such technologies in the

Energy and Utilities sector, which ultimately forces us back to reliance on current law and regulation.

Infrastructure and the Built Environment

The construction and property sectors are also undergoing a transformation with the steady implementation of artificial intelligence and machine learning solutions, part of the innovation wave collectively grouped under the "*Proptech*" banner. As with the Energy and Utility sector, there is no consistent drive to regulate adoption of the technology, given the range of applications it could potentially influence, rather we must look to (or at least have an appreciation of) the impact of adoption in relation to specific areas, when mapped against existing laws and regulations.

There are three growing areas in the construction and property sectors where machine learning tools are beginning to make their mark. The first is in relation to automated building information modelling which is typically applied during the construction of a building, the second is in relation to so-called *Smart Cities* and the third is in relation to facilities management.

Building Information Modelling

Building information modelling (or BIM) tools put simply allow the automation of complex design and modelling when preparing architectural plans for a new building. Such tools enable construction professionals to more accurately and efficiently make use of materials (through for example automated computation of loading stresses); refine construction processes to optimise routing of utilities (such as power and water) and enhance green or environmental profiles (through for example maximal space efficiency and configuration). Machine learning tools enhance BIM by the introduction of predictive and classification capabilities – identifying where components and/or materials selected are incorrect or missing or predicting (by reference to the immediate context of the proposed building) where prior conditions have been deemed to be unsafe.

From a regulatory and legal compliance perspective BIM tools clearly have the potential to enhance safety when constructing buildings but equally speaking blind reliance on such tools will not absolve the user from liability should they fail. As noted elsewhere in this book and in other contexts, it is for the user to re-assure themselves that the tool has the appropriate level of accreditation and certification and to bear in mind that all of the previous issues we have discussed in relation to the inherent "black box" nature of machine learning solutions also applies equally here.

Smart Cities

The term Smart City refers to the smart or intelligent management of municipal infrastructure through the use of technologies such as artificial intelligence and IoT or internet of things. Smart Cities optimise connectivity (so called *hyperconnectivity*) between city infrastructure and buildings, as well as autonomous vehicles and the city's human visitors and residents. I mention this for completeness here only as the implications of such smart infrastructure are far more wide-ranging than artificial intelligence – however that technology has a key part to play in optimising the operational management of such municipalities.

Facilities Management

The final area in the property sector which is being influenced by artificial intelligence is in the provision of facilities management or FM solutions. Clearly the provision of services to any large building is highly labour intensive and therefore ripe for automation. Some examples of this might include *security systems* – using AI to monitor facilities and permit access to buildings; *cleaning and maintenance* – deploying automated solutions (including drones or robots) to clean internal and external surfaces and to spot and/or predict where maintenance to the building is needed; *reception services* – dealing with visitors to the building and handing off to appropriate hosts; and *logistics and waste management* – managing deliveries to the building and removing refuse. The other area where machine learning solutions can benefit use of buildings is by the optimisation of space (through the identification of underutilisation or overutilisation) in particular in a business environment where hot desking is the norm. All of these solutions now exist in a commercial form to a greater or lesser degree. For a wider discussion on robotic process outsourcing, which will be relevant to this section, please see Chapter nine.

CHAPTER NINE
ROBOTIC PROCESS OUTSOURCING
AND ARTIFICIAL INTELLIGENCE AS
A SERVICE (AIAAS)

Robotic Process Outsourcing

Robotic process outsourcing, or robotic process automation ("**RPO**") is not a new concept – it refers to the deployment of automation, whether that be robots or other machines, to replace humans in task-based processes. Typically, RPOs have a hybrid characteristic in that they tend to deliver managed services through a combination of human workers with an automated element.

Industries such as manufacturing have been using progressively complex degrees of automation since the time of the industrial revolution in the early 19th century. Robotic assembly of motor vehicles was pioneered in the mid to late 1960s with the use of spot welding robots by General Motors, quickly followed by more flexible and microprocessor-controlled units in the mid-1970s. By the mid-1980s the industry had been transformed.

What machine learning brings to robotic process outsourcing is the ability for robots to assume significantly more complex tasks to those that have previously been undertaken. To continue the car manufacturing analogy, many such robots are now semi-autonomous, with degrees of environment processing, enabling flexible interaction with a changing environment that are at least equivalent to the autonomous vehicles currently being launched on the driving market.

We should not however confine our perspective to manufacturing. Machine learning is opening markets to RPO that have hitherto only been able to be automated on a limited basis, such as the provision of semi-professional tasks involving a high degree of human interaction – front office skills such as call centre and helpdesk operatives for example. The prediction is that ultimately professional level skills will be open to automation, such as those currently practiced by lawyers and accountants.

There are real and complex political and moral arguments at play with ever increasing waves of automation, and the workplace is under a degree of existential threat in the mid to near future the likes of which have not been seen since the industrial revolution. This is a book however about the practical legal consequences of the deployment of such technology. In this sense, outside the other issues that we have analysed in this book, these disruptive considerations are no more different (or at least equivalent to) the considerations that have to be managed when outsourcing in the traditional sense.

Conventional outsourcing, for the uninitiated, entails the transfer of an internally managed service or operation to an external service provider. When introducing automation and artificial intelligence into the workplace, what therefore are the primary practical legal consequences that need to be borne in mind? The first and by far away the most significant consideration is the management of workforce displacement.

Typically in a conventional outsourcing carried out within the UK (and indeed the wider EU), when a service is outsourced, the rights embodied in the EU's Transfers of Undertakings Directive[1] and enacted in the UK under the Transfer of Undertakings (Protection of Employment) Regulations 2006[2]. Broadly speaking, this stipulates that (unlike many jurisdictions where employment is *"at will"*, such as the United States), when an *"undertaking"*[3] is transferred from customer to service provider (a *"relevant transfer"*), the employment of those

---

1 2001/23/EC

2 SI 2006/246

3 There is much UK and EU law on what constitutes an undertaking, but essentially this is the business operation engaged in economic activities which is to be transferred to the service provider, see further *Höfner & Elser v. Macrotron GmbH [1991] ECR I-1979*

employees carrying out the service immediately prior to the transfer is carried over to the service provider, without any break in continuity, thus preserving their extant employment rights. This means that the service provider must continue their employment on equivalent terms. Any dismissals carried out because of a relevant transfer are deemed to be unfair unless there is an *economic, technical* or *organisational* reason for the dismissals which for the purposes of the legislation[4] are deemed to justified. In such circumstances, the affected employee is considered to be redundant and may be entitled to statutory compensation if they have been employed for a continuous period of more than two years[5].

Plainly in the case of robotic displacement, there is no transfer of undertaking, no continuity of employment and redundancy or redeployment of the affected employees is the only option available to the employer. The Employment Rights Act provides as follows: "*For the purposes of this Act an employee who is dismissed shall be taken to be dismissed by reason of redundancy if the dismissal is wholly or mainly attributable to— (a) the fact that his employer has ceased or intends to cease—(i) to carry on the business for the purposes of which the employee was employed by him, or (ii) to carry on that business in the place where the employee was so employed, or (b) the fact that the requirements of that business—(i) for employees to carry out work of a particular kind, or (ii) for employees to carry out work of a particular kind in the place where the employee was employed by the employer, have ceased or diminished or are expected to cease or diminish.*"[6]. The Act continues with the following embellishment: "*In subsection (1) "cease" and "diminish" mean cease and diminish either permanently or temporarily and for whatever reason.*"[7].

---

4 See the Employment Rights Act 1996, s98(2)(c)

5 s135 Employment Rights Act 1996

6 s139(1) Employment Rights Act 1996

7 s139(6) Employment Rights Act 1996

Somewhat perversely this does mean that in terms of justifying grounds for redundancy, the law makes it demonstrably easier to do so in circumstances where a machine is to replace a person.

Whether this will ultimately lead to a public policy change in the event of widespread displacement remains to be seen – already there has been some debate in the UK and the USA about the introduction of a "*workplace automation*" tax, to help fund the retraining of displaced employees. South Korea has taken the first tentative steps on this path by implementing an indirect tax on workplace automation by applying in effect a reduced tax incentive benefit to workplaces originally designed to boost productivity[8]. Somewhat more radically, some economists have suggested going further and have advocated the introduction of a universal basic income as a solution to the inequality and inevitable work displacement caused by the emergence of robots and artificial intelligence[9].

Outside of workplace displacement, what are the other problematic issues which will need to be resolved when outsourcing to artificial intelligence?

Many of these will revolve around the nature of the task and duties which have been delegated. As has been apparent throughout previous chapters of this book – there are going to be specific duties and responsibilities which cannot yet be transferred to a machine learning system because the law has not yet developed a coherent theory of artificial *personhood*. This is likely to be a hugely important step if we are to confer onto machines the responsibility to make decisions which have real (ie. legal and moral) consequences for human beings. Until the law evolves in this way, ultimately what can be outsourced will necessarily be con-

---

8   See http://www.koreatimes.co.kr/www/news/tech/2017/08/133_234312.html
   "Korea takes first step to introduce 'Robot Tax'"

9   The suggestion was made by professor Sir Christopher Pissarides, a Nobel laureate and the Regius professor at the London School of Economics during the World Economic Forum in Davos, 20th January 2016

strained, and we will be left with activities and tasks that are not (or are at least, minimally) regulated.

Aside from these considerations, outsourcing agreements contain a variety of supplier focussed contractual obligations and liabilities to be managed which in theory could be extended to artificially intelligent systems – although some thought would need to be given to their application. Many of the areas which are likely to be applicable have already been discussed at length elsewhere in this book. These include the compliance issues around big data analytics (see the commentary in Chapter three) and the protection and management of intellectual property, both in relation to deliverables created by the machine learning system in the course of the provision of the outsourced services (which as we discussed previously would likely be covered, certainly in the UK by the machine generated copyright provisions of the Copyright, Designs and Patents Act 1988[10]) and in respect of the machine learning system itself (again, see the commentary in Chapter four). Consideration would also need to be given to ongoing service management and Service Level agreements (or SLAs) as these are a feature of most traditional outsourcing agreements. As the name implies, these enforce mandated levels of service performance upon suppliers to ensure that the services being performed do not drop below a particular standard. Whereas in traditional outsourcing agreements these typically are focussed on *direct performance by the supplier of the services*, there is an increasing trend in complex RPOs for these to translate to *maintenance and support of the AI system performing the service*, as these are typically the non-AI (human based) services which are performed in an RPO context and which can be enforced in a traditional manner. Interestingly, in terms of SLA and contract enforcement in RPO there is a potential role to play here for another upcoming technology, so called block-chain enabled *"smart contract"* systems. Initiatives such as the Accord Project[11] an international working party made up of several law firms and technology businesses are looking to develop open source technology standards to transition contracts from static documents into

---

10 See s178 of the CDPA 1988 and s9(3) respectively

11 See https://www.accordproject.org/

fully integrated components of commercial systems – which would mean for example – automatic deduction or "netting off" of service credits in the event that a particular service level was not met, without human intervention.

Artificial Intelligence as a Service (AIaaS)

One of the biggest blocks to date to small and medium sized enterprise in the deployment of machine learning systems and tools has been the level of investment and expertise that is required to successfully build and train such systems. Unsurprisingly this requires a degree of specialist skill that is beyond the means of most in the SME sector and possibly even some larger businesses – it is also in many cases, "*non-core*" in terms of business objectives.

Coupled with this has been a strong trend in the outsourcing market, driven by ubiquity in cloud computing, to move away from traditional "*on premise*" solutions to service based "*on demand*" SasS (Software as a Service) solutions or Cloud based architecture for the delivery of complex managed services.

As machine learning systems become ever more complex and capable we are seeing in turn a complex re-imagining and commoditisation of service delivery related tools and products and the emergence of artificial intelligence as a service or "AIaaS". What AIaaS attempts to offer is a commoditised cognitive computing platform, delivered via the cloud, that allows businesses to leverage the power of pre-built and trained machine learning solutions, either directly, or as part of a robotic process outsourcing via a third party.

AIaaS solutions are broadly speaking structured either as data, compute or pre-packaged services. AIaaS data solutions provide the convenience of ready-made pools of data to enable fast and effective training of machine learning models for common or generic problems – these might for example be comprised of masses of facial images for facial recognition applications. Compute services enable common infrastructural computing tasks to be carried out that are closely integrated with machine learning solutions – such as batch processing. Pre-packaged AIaaS allows for the provision of ready-made AI applications on demand that can be integrated into enterprise offerings.

Use of AIaaS solutions, whether pre-packaged or via data or compute models clearly brings convenience and speed of implementation to many "standard" machine learning solutions, such as facial recognition, language translation or natural language processing. However from a legal perspective such solutions introduce additional levels of difficulty to what may already be a significantly complex RPO arrangement. Numerous issues spring to mind – as a licensee of AIaaS data services you will need to be able to seek sufficient reassurance that the pools of generic data that are provided by the platform provider are sufficiently curated to avoid bias but have not been overfitted. Equally speaking, if you are seeking to include a commoditised application to support a facial recognition application, you will need to have specific assurance that the application has been adequately trained. Disclosure levels and transparency are likely to be key determinants for the customers of AIaaS providers, but equally speaking will prove to be a very difficult interface for the platform providers themselves to navigate, who will be naturally incentivised to keep as much confidential as possible, for fear of giving away valuable proprietary information.

Complex decision making machine learning systems are likely to be harder to manage from a liability perspective if they are dependent upon AIaaS offerings, whether or not they form part of an RPO. Generally speaking, that is because in the event of a contract default – or even circumstances where you need to be able to justify or explain the consequences of a particular decision to an external third party, such as a regulator, you will be faced with having to work back through the licence terms granting access to the AIaaS platform. You will then have to determine the extent to which the provider of the AIaaS cognitive computing platform itself (with all the inherent difficulties we have already discussed in terms of "*black boxes*" and causation) is willing or able to provide an explanation or demonstrate that it is not the cause of the relevant default – not of itself a trivial problem.

As I noted above, AIaaS platforms that are used in this way tend to be heavily proprietary and confidential, and the services they offer are often provided on a *"take it or leave it basis"*. As such it seems unlikely that you will be able to open the lid of the black box and peer inside should something unexpected occur. In fact the licences granted in such circumstances are typically drafted defensively to protect the platform provider.

I would add as a final caveat that we are in the early stages of the evolution of such services. It seems likely that such large platform providers may have to provide a *de minimis* level of transparency in order to establish credibility in their service offers and also to justify their compliance with law and use in regulated contexts.

CHAPTER TEN
ARTIFICIAL INTELLIGENCE
AND CORPORATE LAW

In this chapter on Corporate law we take a closer look at the extent to which machine learning solutions are taking over human duties, both inside and outside the boardroom, whether by direct appointment as directors, or as delegates of the duties owed by directors to their companies and shareholders.

The cybernetic corporation or DAO

Before we look more closely at directors and their duties however, it is worth sketching a picture of the holy grail of automation in a corporate context (or nightmare depending upon your point of view). This is of course the fully cybernetic corporation or DAO (Decentralised Autonomous Corporation). A cybernetic corporation is essentially a corporate machine – where all of the duties of the directors and employees are subsumed and taken over by artificial intelligence and robots undertake all necessary interaction with the physical world – such as fulfilment, logistics and call centre management. DAOs take the concept one stage further and apply blockchain verification technologies to the decisions of such corporatized machines.

Clearly this is the stuff of science fiction and we are not yet at a stage where these entities can exist either in law or in reality (other than in terms of early experimentation) – however there are signs that machine learning is beginning to encroach into corporate governance.

Appointment of artificial intelligence systems as company directors

There are already reports of artificial intelligence systems being "appointed" to boards, either as directors or as observers. In 2016 for example the Nordic financial services company Tieto Corporation appointed the AI Alicia T, as *"a member of its leadership team"* and became the first company in Europe to do so. Tieto however was preceded by Deep Knowledge Ventures in Hong Kong who had in 2014 appointed an AI named Vital (Validating Investment Tool for Advancing Life Sciences) as an *"observer"* over their board of directors.

What then is the current status of artificial intelligence in the boardroom? Could machine learning systems be conceivably appointed as directors?

So far as the law of England and Wales is concerned this question is governed by the Companies Act 2006 rather inconclusively, which provides that *"(1) a private company must have at least one director. (2) a public company must have at least two directors."*[1] and *"(1) a company must have at least one director who is a natural person. (2) this requirement is met if the office of director is held by a natural person as a corporation sole or otherwise by virtue of an office"*[2].

Whilst not explicitly provided for it is evident from its subsequent provisions that the Companies Act only contemplates the appointment of natural and legal persons (ie bodies corporate) as directors. This is because sections 163 and 164 respectively only describe the particulars of natural and legal persons that need to be entered into the company's register of directors.

It appears that so far as AI is concerned, machine learning systems will not (at least in the UK) be entitled to be directly appointed as directors. This is because, as we have previously considered in other contexts, no theory of *artificial personhood* equivalent to legal personality for corporations has yet been developed to confer upon them legal status (for more on this, please see Chapter two under the heading entitled *"Individuation or Artificial Personhood"*).

---

1   Section 154 of the Companies Act 2006

2   Section 155 of the Companies Act 2006

The next question to consider in terms of immediate impact in the boardroom is the extent to which the use of machine learning in a corporate governance context is permitted when one takes into account the fiduciary and statutory duties which are owed by directors to the boards of the companies they are appointed to.

Delegation

Before we discuss the duties themselves, it is probably worth looking briefly at the extent to which directors can delegate those duties – as this will be of immediate relevance to our discussion. Table A (the model form of articles of association prescribed under UK companies legislation[3]) allows directors the ability to delegate their duties as follows: " *(1) Subject to the articles, the directors may delegate any of the powers which are conferred on them under the articles— (a) to such person or committee; (b) by such means (including by power of attorney); (c) to such an extent; (d) in relation to such matters or territories; and (e) on such terms and conditions; as they think fit. (2) If the directors so specify, any such delegation may authorise further delegation of the directors' powers by any person to whom they are delegated. (3) The directors may revoke any delegation in whole or part, or alter its terms and conditions"*[4]. It seems apparent then that so far as delegation is concerned, the law simply does not contemplate these duties being taken over by anything other than a legal or natural person or committee. We are effectively in the same position we discussed earlier in the context of the direct appointment of AIs as directors. Unless there is an evolution to grant some form of artificial personhood to machine learning solutions, this will not be possible. This does not prevent of course artificial intelligence being used in the context of corporate governance – merely that if it is used, the legal basis will have little more significance than if a director used an ordinary computer in the context of his or her duties – AI in essence in this sense becomes transparent and is relegated to a tool or instrumental

---

3 See the Companies (Model Articles) Regulations 2008

4 See article 5 of the Model Articles for companies limited by shares

extension to be utilised. The individual director remains, in these circumstances, fully accountable and responsible for his or her acts.

Director's general duties

So far as the duties themselves are concerned, the Companies Act sets out several key "general" duties – as previously stated in different contexts, I don't propose to list them all here, but rather to concentrate on the ones which may be potentially significant in relation to the use of machine learning. These are the three general duties which are relevant – to *promote the success of the company* (to behave in a way most likely to promote the success of the company)[5]; to *exercise independent judgment*[6]; and to *exercise reasonable care, skill and diligence*[7].

Evidently there is already sufficient anecdotal evidence in the market to suggest that the effective deployment of machine learning solutions in the enterprise can have very beneficial effects in terms of optimising performance and efficiency.

As use of machine learning becomes more and more widespread and such systems become more and more capable it seems likely that the need for directors to advocate the use of such tools within their corporations in order to *promote the success of the company* is likely to grow and that this duty will become commensurately stronger. What is interesting however is that in large part much of the usefulness of machine learning solutions lies in their ability to predict or to provide real-time analysis in relation to a particular situation – in short a *judgmental view*, and potentially the ability to do this more accurately than any human being. It would seem therefore that this has the very real potential to conflict with the other duty I have called out above, the need to *exercise independent judgment*. This duty was originally created to prevent bias

---

5   Section 172 Companies Act 2006

6   Section 173 Companies Act 2006

7   Section 174 Companies Act 2006

or narrow partisanship on the part of a director and his or her decisions – being beholden to one stakeholder or interest or their appointing shareholder at the expense of all others was unlikely to further the over-arching interests of the company in a good sense – but equally speaking one can see how blind adherence to the decisions of a machine learning system, without necessarily exercising a critical review or promoting an alternative approach could also cause a director to fall into the same trap.

There is of course, a similar tautology in relation to the last of the director's duties that we discuss in this chapter – that of *exercising reasonable skill, care and diligence*. Again one can see how the duty might promote increased use of artificial intelligence in the boardroom if it leads to more efficient, rounded and evaluated decisions – in effect enhancing skill and diligence. Misapplied however, it might lead to a completely contrary result and ultimately breach of that duty. As in previous discussions in this book, context, use and application are critical to the successful deployment and utilisation of AI.

Transactional considerations – automated due diligence

Corporate transactions are of course an important feature of this legal landscape – companies and ownership are not static and invariably they will be subject to mergers, acquisitions, divestments and re-organisations. Machine learning has a role to play in this environment as well – principally around one of the key activities involved in any such deal – the corporate due diligence exercise. Typically this involves a detailed analysis and investigation of all of the debts, liabilities and assets of the corporate entity that is either being sold, purchased or merged – usually the exercise is split into three different parts – *financial* which focusses on verifying the financial information provided by the counterparty and to assess the underlying performance of the business; *commercial* which considers the market in which the target business sits and the potential competitive landscape; and *legal* which considers all of the legal elements of the transaction. This might cover for example the contracts that the business holds from customers; employment contracts with key employees; real property documentation such as leases; critical supply agreements into the business; how any intellectual property assets might be held and any actual or pending litigation.

Machine learning solutions are becoming more ubiquitous in relation to financial and legal due diligence exercises, leading many journalists of hyperbolic predisposition to prematurely predict the end of either lawyers or accountants or both. What these solutions do is ingest and filter the relevant financial or legal information on an automated basis into a pre-structured due diligence report. Typically this avoids the need for armies of junior lawyers or accountants to review the information manually to produce the same digest.

Generally speaking, automating the due diligence process also allows for significant increases in speed (machine learning solutions tend to be quicker than human beings) and decreases in cost (machine learning solutions are not paid by the hour as are legal or financial professionals but are subject to a licensing fee which tends to be much lower). There are therefore significant and apparent business benefits to introducing these processes into corporate transactions – I would however strike a note of caution and ask you the reader to cast your mind back to the contents of Chapter one. All machine learning based artificial intelligence requires significant and competent training in order to achieve good results. If the automated due diligence system that is deployed in a particular transaction has not been trained properly then the result it produces will at best be poor and at worst plain wrong. Given the professional duties that are owed by both accountancy firms and law firms to their clients – and in particular to act in the client's best interests, and also the potential for clients to initiate professional misconduct proceedings, it would seem sensible as a basic minimum to ensure that proper steps have been taken to verify that any machine learning system which is used has been properly tested and trained. In many cases it may actually be sensible for the professional advisor to go one step further and double check the actual automated due diligence report produced (which may perversely completely undermine the business rationales of speed and cost discussed earlier). I would suggest that the worst course of conduct is to accept any such report *"in blind faith"*.

CHAPTER ELEVEN
MANAGING MACHINE LEARNING
SYSTEMS ON A PRACTICAL BASIS

In this final chapter, I attempt to provide some further practical considerations for selected areas of the law that we have discussed in this book.

Causation (Chapter two)

Given the current state of the law, there is little that can be recommended on a practical basis in relation to the causative issues created by artificial intelligence.

One consideration in a contractual context might be to investigate with your counterparty the extent to which insurance is available to cover any potential liability issues created by the relevant machine learning system. If such insurance is available, then I would suggest you look beyond the level of the cover and take a more forensic view of what the relevant insurer defines as a "*fault*" or a "*defect*" – remember that machine learning solutions do occasionally manifest *edge case* decisions or actions which are at the margins of what might ordinarily be treated as reasonable. These may not be explicable on a human basis but do not necessarily indicate an operational fault or defect on the part of the system.

Big Data and the GDPR (Chapter three)

In Chapter three we learned that artificial intelligence, or at least machine learning solutions, are particularly problematic when applied to the regulatory regime created by the General Data Protection Regulation or GDPR.

In terms of identifying particular ways forward, it is worth reiterating the basic pitfalls again. Machine learning solutions are particularly opaque in their computational processing methods so will require additional (and innovative) effort to clear the "*transparency*" hurdle set out by the privacy information notice requirements of the GDPR. As we saw in Chapter three, this might be achieved by use of icons (ie. a form of systemised iconography), "*just in time*" notifications (such as pop ups) or "*layering*" (ie. allowing for progressively more information to be disclosed when clicking a "*learn more*" link).

If your AI system is intended to process personal data it should at the outset be designed with the goal privacy at its heart. If in addition your system also includes profiling or automated decision making, in circumstances where such profiling or automated decision making produces "*legal effects which significantly affect data subjects*"[1] without meaningful human intervention, you will **not** be able to rely on the legitimate interests ground for lawfulness of processing and will need instead to rely on proactive lawful consent as a ground, with all of the potential issues (including withdrawal) which such an approach brings. A practical approach here necessitates the introduction of real (rather than token) human oversight at some level or an assessment that the processing does not produce significant or meaningful legal effects.

In either case any such position will need to be supported by comprehensive privacy assessments to gauge the scale and nature of the impact on data subjects. The key requirement must be to define the strategic case for use of the relevant AI system such that it can be justified to the data subjects it affects ethically as of demonstrable benefit to them. The undoubted complexity and innovation of such systems needs to be balanced against the *need* for their use. Could the same end goals be achieved without the use of such systems. In short are they essential or a nice-to-have?

Finally, post-Brexit, consideration will need to be given to the new data related offences that are likely to created by the Data Protection Act. Specifically sufficient assurances should be obtained from the developers of any AI or machine learning system that you plan to use, together

---

1   See Article 22 GDPR

with appropriate complementary endorsement from your lawyers that use of the system will not create criminal liability for you or your organ-isation.

Intellectual Property (Chapter four)

Unless working on open-source or open access style initiatives, developers of machine learning solutions should give consideration to making the process of developing and training their systems as confid-ential and proprietary as possible to avail of protection under the new EU Trade Secrets Directive when that is implemented into national law. In the US, equivalent legislation already exists[2].

This will entail putting in place procedures for relevant employees (such as non-disclosure agreements) and enhancing physical and logical security measures. As noted above, these considerations should be applied not just to the development of the appropriate machine learning software model but also the training process, including the curated data sets and methodologies that are used to train the systems.

Licensing in data sets for either training or operational use will need to be managed carefully to avoid falling into the *learned behaviours paradigm* we discuss in Chapter four. This means making allowance for *information residuals* (as described in Chapter four, these are *not* the contents of the data sets themselves but rather the associative and correl-ative aspects describing statistical patterns and correlations in data used by the system which cause the learner element of the system to adapt and improve its outputs).

---

2   See the Uniform Trade Secrets Act

Avoiding Bias (Chapter five)

You should ensure that proper investigative steps are taken to understand the nature and quality of the data sets provided to the machine learning system before you deploy it in a real-life situation. Unless your application is to be trained on an unsupervised basis, remember that simply having access to a huge data lake of information will not necessarily guarantee quality outputs or outputs relevant to your application. Equally speaking you need to ensure that the data are not too limited by *overfitting*.

A clear understanding of the methodology involved in curating the relevant data set needs to be obtained, and if human equivalent skills are being translated into a machine context, sufficient identification of the skill levels of the relevant individuals involved should also be sought.

Competition and Trade (Chapter seven)

Whether your machine learning solution is pro-competitive or anti-competitive will depend largely on the trade context involved.

Be mindful of potentially anti-competitive implications if you are operating in a monopolistic or oligopolistic environment or are likely to do so (if for example you are first onto the market with a new machine learning application that is likely to be very disruptive to a traditional market sector). If in doubt, seek the advice of competent competition lawyers.

Artificial Intelligence as a Service (Chapter nine)

The considerations that we have discussed above in relation to causation, big data, intellectual property and bias are all likely to be relevant in the circumstances where you are contemplating the licensing in of an AIaaS service as a user. Getting comfortable with the training methodologies used by the AIaaS offering is a key part of establishing transparency within the solution, assurance and verifying applicable quality levels. AIaaS platforms that are reluctant to offer this reassurance should be challenged where possible and practicable.

I would suggest also that given that AIaaS services tend to be integrated into wider RPO offerings, which may or may not include a number of different suppliers, you should make absolutely certain (irrespective of whether such can be proven) that any liability can at least in theory be traced back through appropriate licensing arrangements to the relevant AIaaS platform provider. Understanding how their insurers propose to cover risks caused by their platform will also be crucial – in this case, as noted above, it is important to look beyond levels of cover and examine the *nature* of the insurance coverage. Of course if you are an AIaaS platform provider then you should potentially consider how to limit your exposure in such circumstances – a diametrically opposite objective!

From an intellectual property perspective, if you are providing data to an AIaaS platform for a compute or pre-packaged application, you should consider how the AIaaS platform will retain your data or information residuals, which may or may not be legislated for in the applicable licensing agreement. The aggregation or pooling of per-sonally identifiable information or PII from multiple customers is not something that is advisable (or indeed permissible) under the GDPR, but where personal data is not involved this might be being considered. Alternatives to data aggregation might be insisting on a "*walled garden*" approach, but you will need to trade off the performance benefits of exposing the machine learning solution to wider data sets in return for increased security.

Accessing AIaaS for data services (ie pre-modelled and curated data sets) will necessitate (as previously discussed elsewhere) a full understanding of how representative and accurate that data set actually is.

Corporate governance and transactional management (Chapter ten)

Until some element of legal personality or artificial personhood is granted to artificial intelligence, appointing such systems directly to boards of companies will not be possible.

As we saw in Chapter ten, even formally delegating the performance of director's duties is likely to be problematic in the UK under the current Companies Act until the issue of personhood is settled. The model form of articles of association for companies guaranteed by shares contemplates delegation to a person or a committee. It may be worthwhile considering an amendment to your articles of association to clarify that directors can consult with and otherwise use artificially intelligent machines in the course of discharging their duties – but obviously any such language will be clarificatory only and will not absolve directors ultimately of their duties and responsibilities.

Finally, so far as automated due diligence reports are concerned – be careful not to accept these at face value – as with the summary section on bias above – make sure you are comfortable with and understand the methodologies used to train the system that has produced the automated report.

MORE BOOKS BY
LAW BRIEF PUBLISHING

A selection of our other titles available now:

'Occupiers, Highways and Defective Premises Claims: A Practical Guide Post-Jackson – 2nd Edition' by Andrew Mckie
'A Practical Guide to Financial Ombudsman Service Claims' by Adam Temple & Robert Scrivenor
'A Practical Guide to the Law of Enfranchisement and Lease Extension' by Paul Sams
'A Practical Guide to Marketing for Lawyers – 2nd Edition' by Catherine Bailey & Jennet Ingram
'A Practical Guide to Advising Schools on Employment Law' by Jonathan Holden
'Certificates of Lawful Use and Development: A Guide to Making and Determining Applications' by Bob Mc Geady & Meyric Lewis
'A Practical Guide to the Law of Dilapidations' by Mark Shelton
'A Practical Guide to the 2018 Jackson Personal Injury and Costs Reforms' by Andrew Mckie
'A Guide to Consent in Clinical Negligence Post-Montgomery' by Lauren Sutherland QC
'A Practical Guide to Running Housing Disrepair and Cavity Wall Claims: 2nd Edition' by Andrew Mckie & Ian Skeate
'A Practical Guide to the General Data Protection Regulation (GDPR)' by Keith Markham
'A Practical Guide to Digital and Social Media Law for Lawyers' by Sherree Westell
'A Practical Guide to Holiday Sickness Claims – 2nd Edition' by Andrew Mckie & Ian Skeate
'A Practical Guide to Inheritance Act Claims by Adult Children Post-Ilott v Blue Cross' by Sheila Hamilton Macdonald
'A Practical Guide to Elderly Law' by Justin Patten

'Arguments and Tactics for Personal Injury and Clinical Negligence Claims'
by Dorian Williams

'A Practical Guide to QOCS and Fundamental Dishonesty' by James Bentley

'A Practical Guide to Drone Law' by Rufus Ballaster, Andrew Firman, Eleanor Clot

'Practical Mediation: A Guide for Mediators, Advocates, Advisers, Lawyers, and
Students in Civil, Commercial, Business, Property, Workplace, and
Employment Cases' by Jonathan Dingle with John Sephton

'Practical Horse Law: A Guide for Owners and Riders' by Brenda Gilligan

'A Comparative Guide to Standard Form Construction and Engineering Contracts'
by Jon Close

'A Practical Guide to Compliance for Personal Injury Firms Working With Claims
Management Companies' by Paul Bennett

'A Practical Guide to the Landlord and Tenant Act 1954: Commercial Tenancies'
by Richard Hayes & David Sawtell

'A Practical Guide to Personal Injury Claims Involving Animals' by Jonathan Hand

'A Practical Guide to Psychiatric Claims in Personal Injury' by Liam Ryan

'Introduction to the Law of Community Care in England and Wales'
by Alan Robinson

'A Practical Guide to Dog Law for Owners and Others' by Andrea Pitt

'Ellis and Kevan on Credit Hire – 5th Edition'
by Aidan Ellis & Tim Kevan

'RTA Allegations of Fraud in a Post-Jackson Era: The Handbook – 2nd Edition'
by Andrew Mckie

'RTA Personal Injury Claims: A Practical Guide Post-Jackson' by Andrew Mckie

'On Experts: CPR35 for Lawyers and Experts' by David Boyle

'An Introduction to Personal Injury Law' by David Boyle

'A Practical Guide to Claims Arising From Accidents Abroad and Travel Claims'
by Andrew Mckie & Ian Skeate

'A Practical Guide to Cosmetic Surgery Claims' by Dr Victoria Handley

'A Practical Guide to Chronic Pain Claims' by Pankaj Madan

'A Practical Guide to Claims Arising from Fatal Accidents' by James Patience

'A Practical Approach to Clinical Negligence Post-Jackson' by Geoffrey Simpson-Scott
'A Practical Guide to Personal Injury Trusts' by Alan Robinson
'Employers' Liability Claims: A Practical Guide Post-Jackson' by Andrew Mckie
'A Practical Guide to Subtle Brain Injury Claims' by Pankaj Madan
'The Law of Driverless Cars: An Introduction' by Alex Glassbrook
'A Practical Guide to Costs in Personal Injury Cases' by Matthew Hoe
'A Practical Guide to Alternative Dispute Resolution in Personal Injury Claims – Getting the Most Out of ADR Post-Jackson' by Peter Causton, Nichola Evans, James Arrowsmith
'A Practical Guide to Personal Injuries in Sport' by Adam Walker & Patricia Leonard
'The No Nonsense Solicitors' Practice: A Guide To Running Your Firm' by Bettina Brueggemann
'Baby Steps: A Guide to Maternity Leave and Maternity Pay' by Leah Waller
'The Queen's Counsel Lawyer's Omnibus: 20 Years of Cartoons from The Times 1993-2013' by Alex Steuart Williams

These books and more are available to order online direct from the publisher at www.lawbriefpublishing.com, where you can also read free sample chapters. For any queries, contact us on 0844 587 2383 or mail@lawbriefpublishing.com.

Our books are also usually in stock at www.amazon.co.uk with free next day delivery for Prime members, and at good legal bookshops such as Hammicks and Wildy & Sons.

We are regularly launching new books in our series of practical day-to-day practitioners' guides. Visit our website and join our free newsletter to be kept informed and to receive special offers, free chapters, etc.

You can also follow us on Twitter at www.twitter.com/lawbriefpub.

Lightning Source UK Ltd.
Milton Keynes UK
UKHW021814030719
345513UK00003B/28/P